IT'S THE GREAT PUMPKIN, CHARLIE BROWN™

IT'S THE GREAT PUMPKIN, CHARLIE BROWN™

The Making of a Television Classic

BY LEE MENDELSON WITH
REFLECTIONS BY BILL MELENDEZ

Schulz

HARPER

NEW YORK · LONDON · TORONTO · SYDNEY

"For Jeannie, Helen, and Ploenta"

HARPER

IT'S THE GREAT PUMPKIN, CHARLIE BROWN:
THE MAKING OF A TELEVISION CLASSIC

IT'S THE GREAT PUMPKIN, CHARLIE BROWN. © 2006 by United Feature Syndicate, Inc. All rights reserved. Peanuts is a registered trademark of United Feature Syndicate, Inc. Printed in the United States of America. No part of this book may be used or reproduced in any manner whatsoever without written permission except in the case of brief quotations embodied in critical articles and reviews. For information address HarperCollins Publishers, 10 East 53rd Street, New York, NY 10022.

HarperCollins books may be purchased for educational, business, or sales promotional use. For information please write: Special Markets Department, HarperCollins Publishers, 10 East 53rd Street, New York, NY 10022.

Designed by Jamie Kerner-Scott

FIRST EDITION

ISBN-10: 0-06-089721-X
ISBN-13: 978-0-06-089721-5

06 07 08 09 10 ❖/QWT 10 9 8 7 6 5 4 3 2 1

http://www.harpercollins.com

CONTENTS

THE GREAT PUMPKIN GOES TO WASHINGTON

On June 7, 2001, Charles Schulz was posthumously awarded the Congressional Gold Medal in the Rotunda of our nation's capitol. Monte, Charles Schulz's son, who accepted the award on behalf of his father, was joined on the dais by the Schulz family and a number of U.S. Senators.

Senator Trent Lott, who had just lost his position that morning as Majority Leader, stood up and said, "Now I know what it feels like when Lucy pulls the

football away from Charlie Brown." It was a scene we had first animated in *It's the Great Pumpkin, Charlie Brown.*

Senator Diane Feinstein also spoke at the ceremony. She said, "Washington can sometimes be a very lonely place, not unlike the pumpkin patch when Linus is waiting for the Great Pumpkin."

When the Marine Corps band entered, first playing the "Great Pumpkin Waltz," and then "Linus and Lucy," there wasn't a dry eye in the house.

For more than 110 years, comic strips have reflected changes in American culture, but no comic artist has ever done so with as much beauty or acuity as Charles Schulz.

And as for the Great Pumpkin, there has probably never been a more original idea in the history of comics. The following is the story of the most famous—though unseen—pumpkin, and how he became part of our national consciousness.

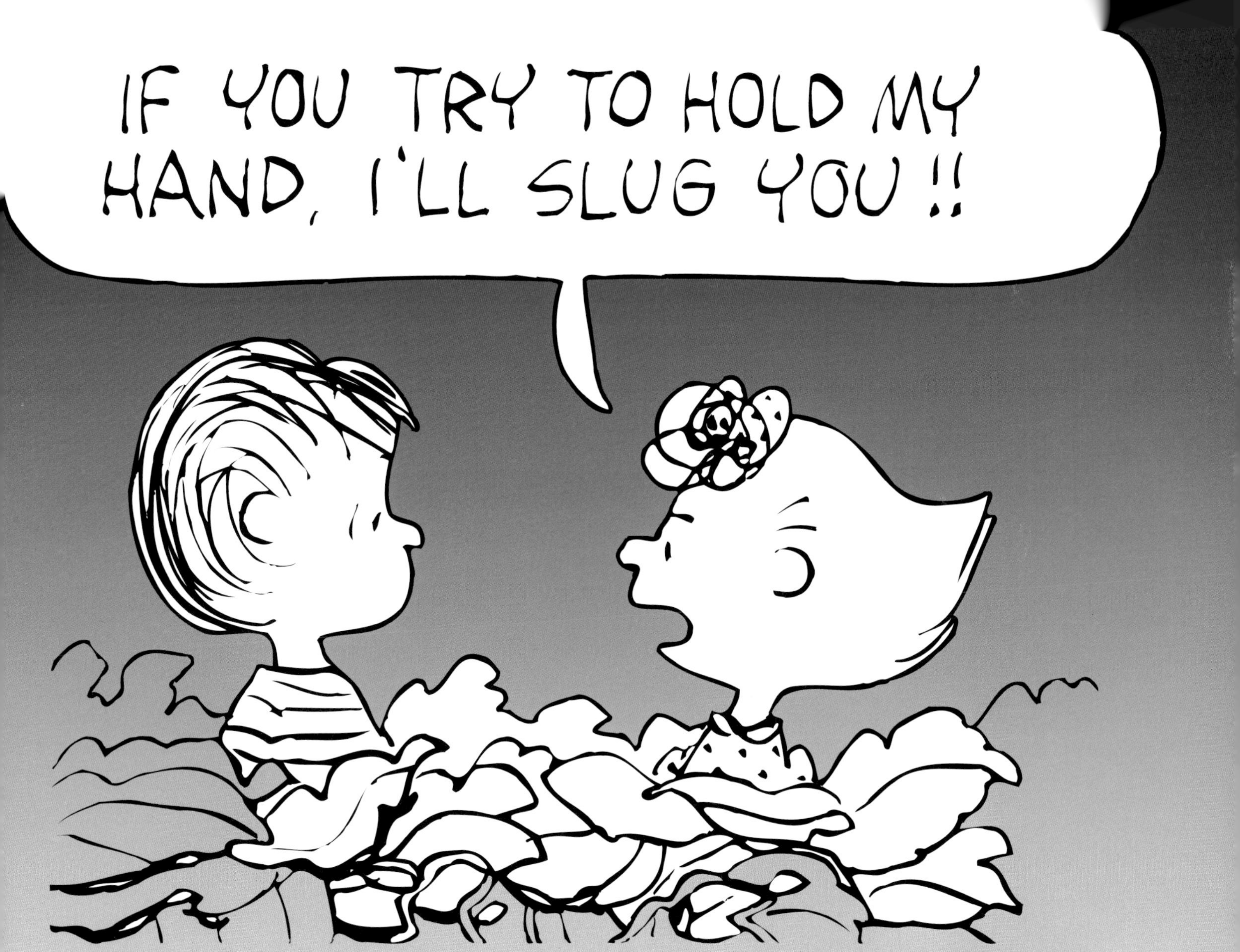
IF YOU TRY TO HOLD MY HAND, I'LL SLUG YOU !!

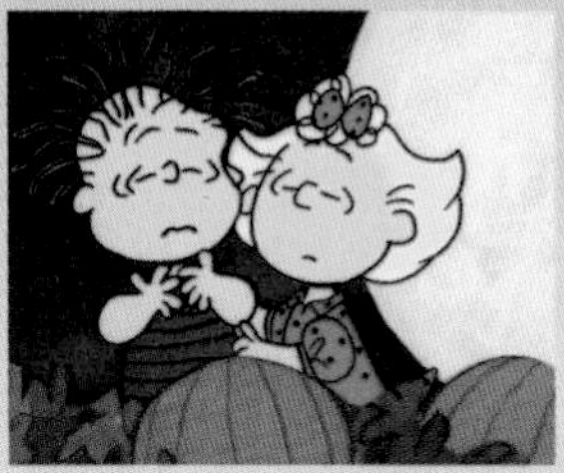

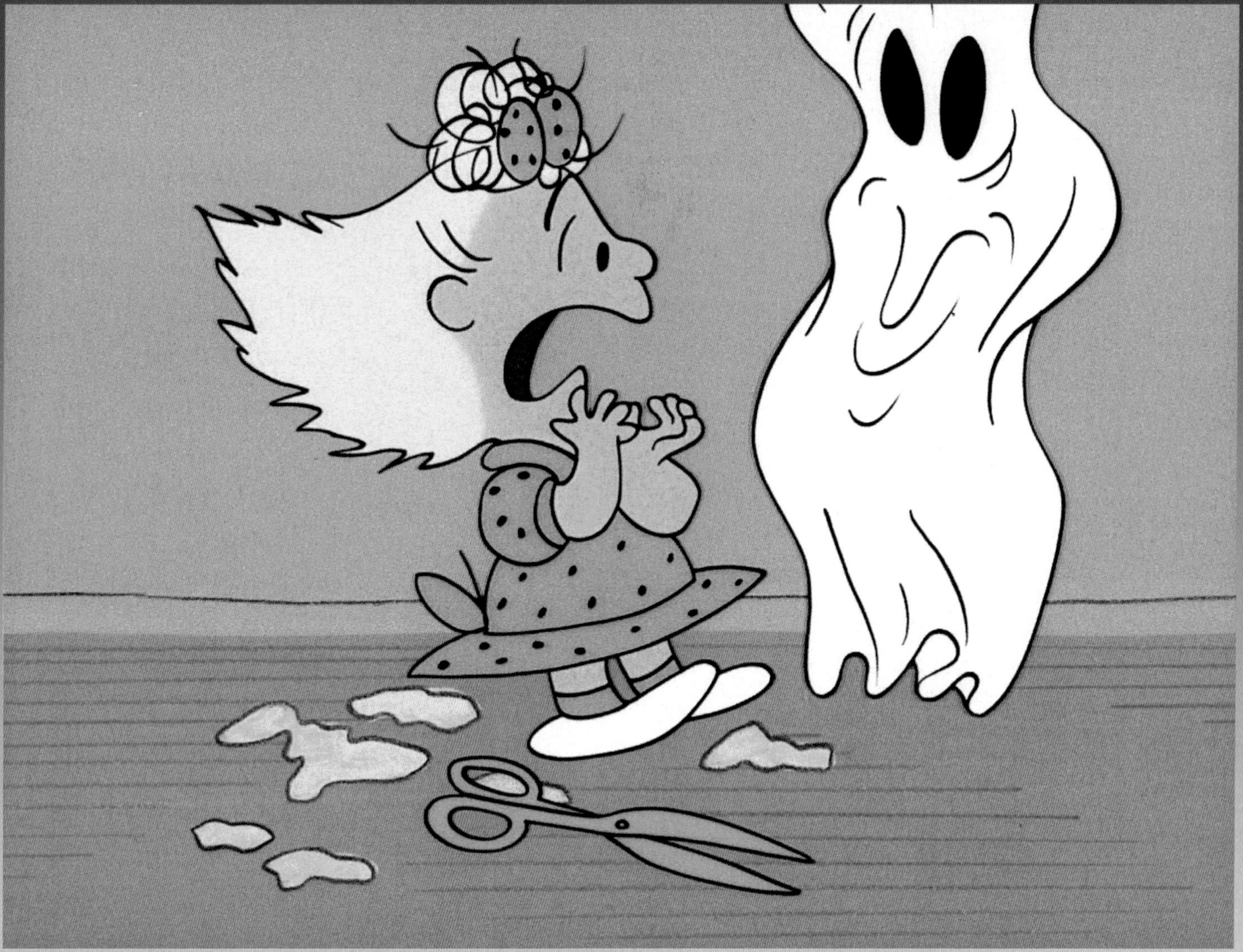

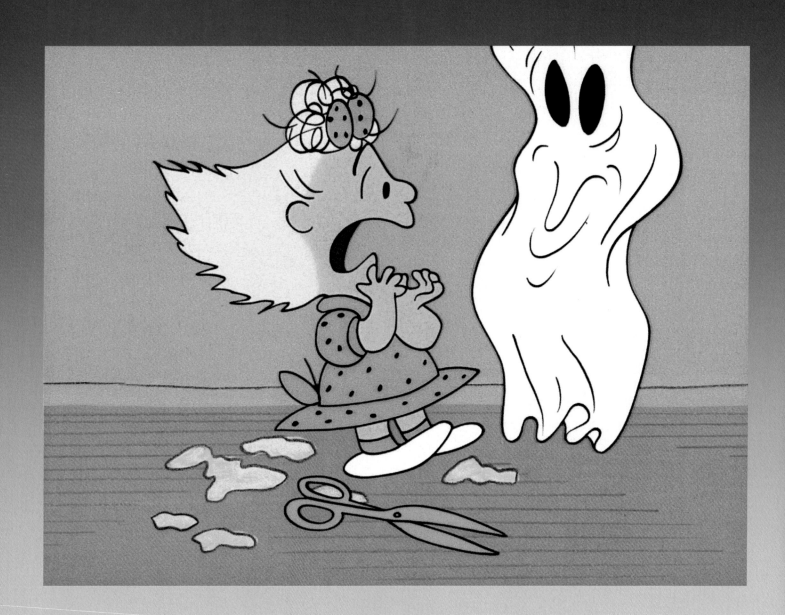

WE NEED ANOTHER BLOCKBUSTER . . . OR ELSE!

As we recounted in our book *A Charlie Brown Christmas: The Making of a Tradition*—after we had finished the show and watched the final screening—animator Bill Melendez and I feared we had ruined Charlie Brown. The special just hadn't turned out the way we had hoped.

My instinct was confirmed when I took the show to the network in New York. The two top executives who viewed it didn't like the show either and said so in no uncertain terms: "Unfortunately this will be the first and last Peanuts special that the network will buy."

Thankfully, when *A Charlie Brown Christmas* debuted on the CBS network on December 9, 1965, it ranked number 2, with a rating of 28.8 and 46.6 per share.

This meant that nearly half of the people watching television that night were tuned in to our show.

The next day one of those same network execs called me and said, "Well, we'd like to buy two more shows . . . with an option on a third . . . but my aunt in New Jersey didn't like it either." Honest, that's what he said!

TRICKS OR TREATS..

Charles Schulz (known as "Sparky" to his friends), Bill Melendez, and I quickly decided that the next special should be about Charlie Brown's terrible baseball team. Baseball had been one of the main themes in *Peanuts*, and so we had a lot of material to start with.

Sparky came up with the idea that a local merchant would offer Charlie Brown uniforms, but when the merchant finds out that Charlie Brown has girls on his team, he tells Charlie Brown he can only have the uniforms if he takes the girls off his team. What an emotional conflict for "poor" Charlie Brown! He has always dreamed of having uniforms, and his worst player is Lucy anyway. Of course he finally decides to pass on the uniforms, out of loyalty to the girls. Sparky was way out in front about girls and sports: the year was 1966, and the issue was just starting to gain national attention.

Even though we were pleased with the show we ultimately created, it was still a bit of a shock when *Charlie Brown's All Stars!* ranked number 1 in the rankings, with 23.8 rating and a 46.1 percent share. Naturally, I assumed we were in pretty good shape when I returned to the network the very next week. But here's how I remember the meeting, with the same "suits" as before . . .

Network Exec: Congratulations. The rating was great. Two in a row. You all must be very excited.

Lee: We can't wait to get started on the next show.

Network Exec: Well that's kind of why we called you in. What do you have in mind for the next one?

Lee: We haven't discussed it yet.

Network Exec: Now don't get me wrong, we're very pleased. But we need another show like *Christmas* . . . you know . . . one that we can run more than once or twice. The baseball show did just fine, but we'll probably run it only one more time. You can't repeat most specials more than once.

Lee: So you want us to . . .

Network Exec: We want you to come up with a *blockbuster* like *Christmas* . . . something we can run every year.

He practically yelled the word "blockbuster."

Lee: A blockbuster.

I looked at the executive, who was all smiles.

Network Exec: Can you guys do it?

Lee: Well, I don't know if anyone can guarantee a blockbuster in this business.

The executive put on his game face. It was clear he wasn't messing around.

Network Exec: Well, you know we've ordered one more show, and we have to be frank here. If we don't get a blockbuster, we may not pick up an option for the fourth show.

Lee: We thought being number one and number two with our first two shows would give you a little confidence in us.

Lee Mendelson holding a still from *It's the Great Pumpkin, Charlie Brown,* with Bill Melendez in 2005

> "So what does one do when one needs a blockbuster . . . a guaranteed blockbuster? One prays and goes to a man named Schulz."

Network Exec: This is a tough racket, kid. You're only as good as your last show. But we do have great confidence in you fellahs, and we think you should be able to come up with another blockbuster.

I laugh when I think how brash I was at age 33.

Lee: Okay. You got it!

Network Exec: Attaboy. Get us an outline in a few weeks.

I left the meeting in a state of disbelief. What I thought would be a celebration turned into a real downer. So what *does* one do when one needs a blockbuster . . . a *guaranteed* blockbuster? One prays and goes to a man named Schulz.

Bill Melendez immediately flew up from Los Angeles, and I met him at the San Francisco airport, just a few minutes from my home. He and I had worked together since 1963, but he and Sparky had begun working together five years before that, doing animated commercials for Ford.

While doing research for our book about *Christmas*, Bill and I discovered that while my great-grandfather was selling clothes to the miners in San Francisco during the Gold Rush in 1851, his grandfather was bringing mules up from Mexico to sell to the miners as well. So there was probably a Mendelson–Melendez connection even way back then.

As we made the one hour drive to Sparky's studio in Sebastopol, Bill was a little more upset about the challenge the network posed to us than I had anticipated. Of all the meetings we had together over the four decades (apart from the Christmas show), this would turn out to be the most crucial one. This would decide whether our winning streak was over or whether we'd have a long career.

I told them the network was thrilled with the ratings on the first two shows.

Sparky: So I assume they want a third one?

Lee: Yes.

Bill: (still annoyed) They want a "blockbuster", like "Christmas."

Sparky (to me): A "blockbuster"?

Lee: Well...that's what they said. Heh, heh.

Sparky: And did you promise them a blockbuster?

Lee: Well I figured 'what the heck'—since I had committed to bringing them and the sponsors (Coca-Cola) a Christmas show last year even before you *had* a Christmas show I might as well just commit to another blockbuster like they wanted and so I did.

Silence. It seemed like hours but it was probably just minutes.

Sparky: What show do you have in mind for this blockbuster?

Lee: I thought *you* could solve that problem, Sparky.

I felt my three-year association with Messrs. Schulz and Melendez slipping away . . .

Sparky: Well, let's do it.

(Those were the exact same glorious words that I had heard from Sparky a year earlier when I called him and said "I think I just sold a Charlie Brown Christmas show.")

"What Christmas show is that?" he asked again, this time as if to charge all of our batteries.

"The one you have to outline tomorrow, because they need it in Atlanta by Monday," I answered sheepishly.

He paused and said, once more, "Let's do it." And he did!)

Charles Schulz was the most determined man I ever met. He loved a challenge of any kind, and he would face it head-on with total confidence. The network, in putting us to the test like that, may have actually done us a favor.

But back to the meeting. Now that we had agreed we would do the show, we needed to come up with the idea—and fast. We were all kind of blankly staring at nothing in particu-

> "Charles Schulz was the most determined man I ever met. He loved a challenge of any kind, and he would face it head-on with total confidence."

lar. Our minds were set on finding a theme. Finally I got up the nerve to speak.

Lee: How about something involving all the unrequited love between Sally and Linus . . . Lucy and Schroeder . . . Charlie Brown and the little red-haired girl . . .

> HERE'S THE WORLD WAR I FLYING ACE REPORTING FOR DUTY

Sparky: That might be kind of tricky.

Bill: How about doing something with those strips you started a few months ago . . . the one with Snoopy as a WWI Flying Ace? Whatever made you think of that?

Sparky: Well, my son Monte thinks it was his idea, though I thought it was mine . . .

Bill: How about doing something with that?

Sparky: Those strips were fun to do. It's too bad he can't actually fly.

Bill stood up with feigned bravado.

BILL: What do you mean he can't fly? I am an *animator*. Of course I can make him fly. I can make him do *anything*!

Bill sat back down and started to sketch out how Snoopy would fly on his doghouse in animated form, and Sparky lit up like a jack-o'-lantern.

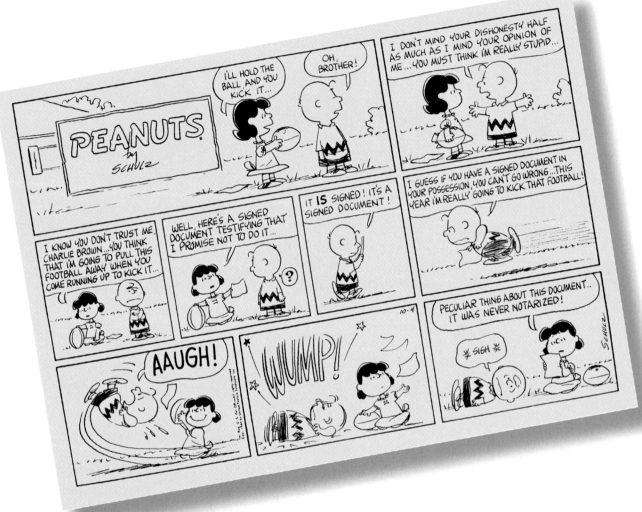

Sparky: That's great. That would make a great scene.

Then there was silence again, as we were wont to have in these meetings. Ideas percolated slowly until, hopefully, a story would evolve. Again, I offered up an idea.

Lee: We haven't animated Lucy pulling the football away.

Lee Mendelson, Bill Melendez, and Charles Schulz

Maybe we can work that in somewhere.

Bill: That would be great to animate. Poor Charlie Brown flying through the air . . . and crashing.

Sparky: Yes. And we need to find something for Schroeder to do again. Some scene with him at the piano like we did in *Christmas* with Vince Guaraldi's great music.

Lee: Snoopy was so funny dancing in *Christmas*. If the Flying

Ace ends up in the show, maybe he could do a dance.

Sparky: You know what? Maybe Schroeder could play some World War I songs, and Snoopy could do something with that. I'd like that a lot.

More silence. The dots hadn't been connected yet. We had a flying scene . . . a piano scene . . . and a football scene.

It was lunchtime so we took a break and had some sandwiches.

It was then that I asked Sparky how he got the idea for the Great Pumpkin.

Sparky thought about it for a few seconds.

Sparky: You know, I've always been kind of ambivalent about Santa Claus.

Lee and Bill: (simultaneously) Santa Claus!!??

Sparky: That's right. First of all, we forget that there are hundreds of thousands of poor kids in this world who are lucky if they get even one or two presents at Christmas time. And here they've heard so much about Santa Claus and all the gifts he delivers. It must be very hard on a lot of families . . . a lot of kids. And, secondly, when a kid finally

finds out that there is no Santa Claus, he must wonder how many other things he has been told that are not true.

Now I may be way off on all this Santa Claus business, and it's not a big deal I guess. But the Great Pumpkin is really a kind of a satire on Santa Claus, because Linus of course writes for gifts and expects to get them. And when the Great Pumpkin doesn't come, Linus is crushed. It shows that you can't always get what you hoped for but you can still survive . . . and you can keep trying. Linus never gives up, just like Charlie Brown.

When lunch was finished, we went back to the new show. For some reason the light bulb still hadn't gone on yet.

OH, GREAT PUMPKIN, PLEASE DON'T LET ME DOWN!

Lee: So we've got some good scenes with the football . . . the Flying Ace . . . and Schroeder.

Sparky: When do they want this show?

Lee: Sometime between October and February. Just as long as it's a blockbuster. Ha, ha.

Sparky: Do you think they would go for a Halloween show?

Lee: I don't know. I don't think there's ever been an animated Halloween show. Do you want me to call them and see?

I called the network and asked them if we could do a Halloween show.

Network Exec: It's up to you guys. Just be sure it's a block—

Lee: (interrupting) I'll call you back later.

I hung up the phone before he could get in another word.

Lee: He says it's up to us.

Sparky: So why don't we do something with Linus and the Great Pumpkin?

Bill and I both jumped up and said: *Yes!!!! That's it!!!*

It was one of those moments when you know something important, creatively, has transpired. It would happen many times for the three of us in the next 38 years.

Sparky: So the whole thing can start off with Linus getting ready in the Pumpkin Patch . . . and then continue with the whole business with getting Sally to come with him.

> " It was one of those moments when you know something important, creatively, has transpired. It would happen many times for the three of us in the next 38 years. "

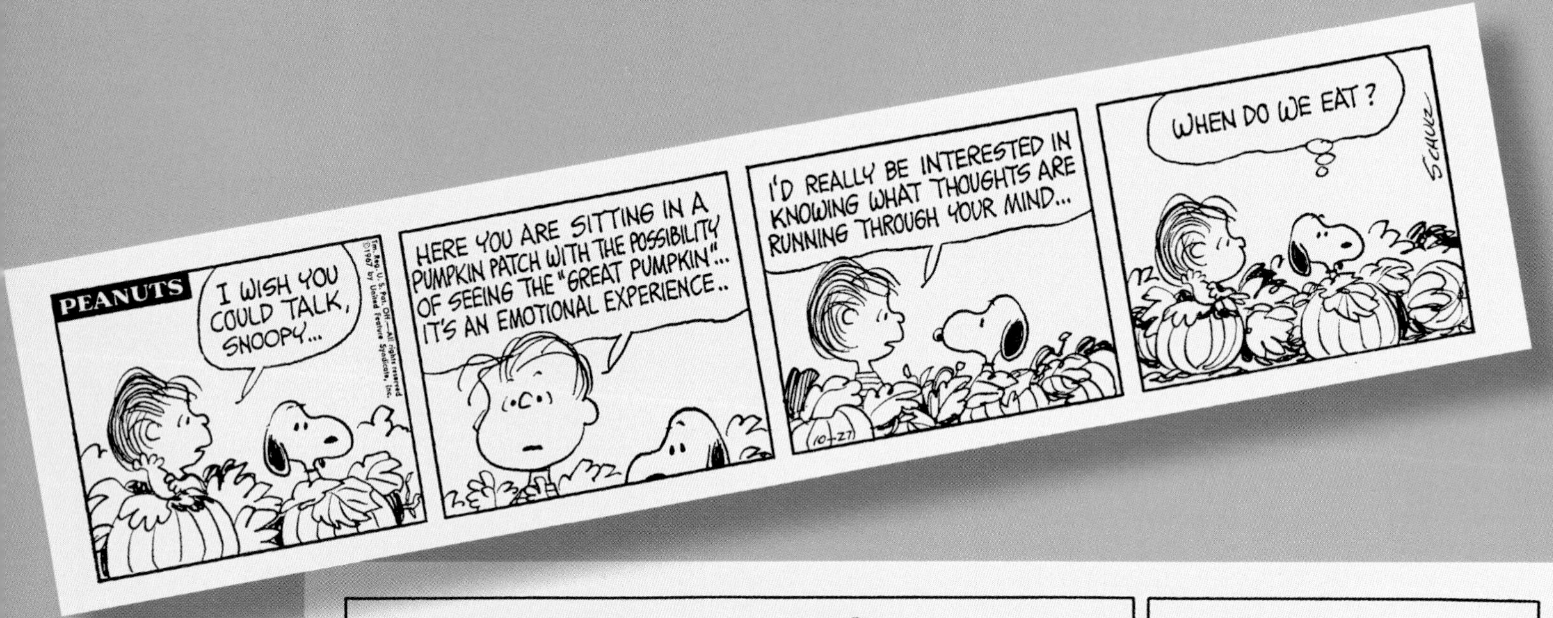
PEANUTS
I WISH YOU COULD TALK, SNOOPY...
HERE YOU ARE SITTING IN A PUMPKIN PATCH WITH THE POSSIBILITY OF SEEING THE "GREAT PUMPKIN"... IT'S AN EMOTIONAL EXPERIENCE..
I'D REALLY BE INTERESTED IN KNOWING WHAT THOUGHTS ARE RUNNING THROUGH YOUR MIND...
10-27
WHEN DO WE EAT ?
SCHULZ

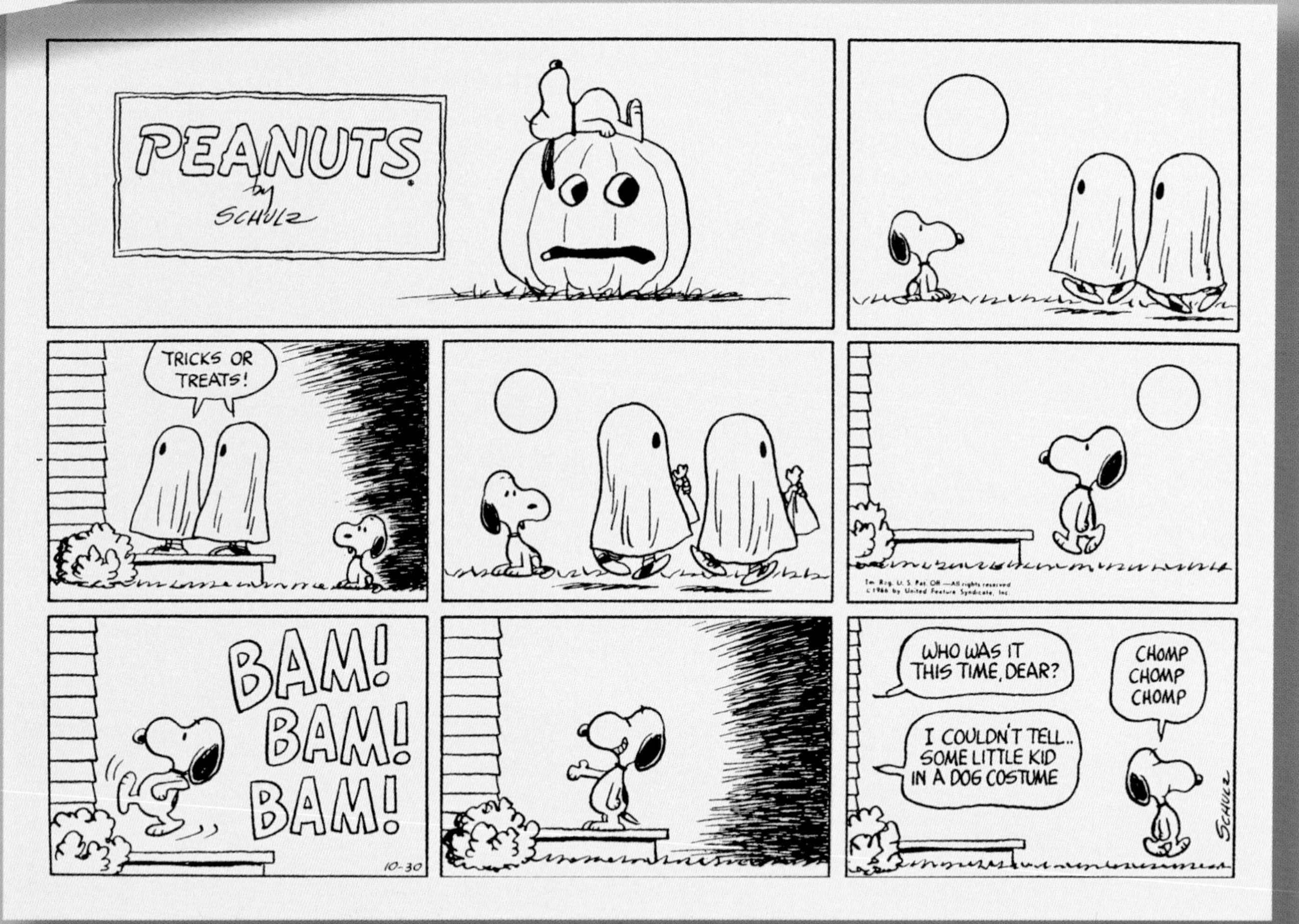
PEANUTS
by
SCHULZ
TRICKS OR TREATS!
BAM! BAM! BAM!
10-30
WHO WAS IT THIS TIME, DEAR?
I COULDN'T TELL.. SOME LITTLE KID IN A DOG COSTUME
CHOMP CHOMP CHOMP
SCHULZ

Lee: Maybe we could have a Halloween party.

Bill: Halloween fits the World War I Flying Ace perfectly. . . .
He looks like he's in costume.

Sparky: We need to add some trick-or-treats.

Bill: That will be great to animate.

NOTHING BUT SINCERITY AS FAR AS THE EYE CAN SEE!

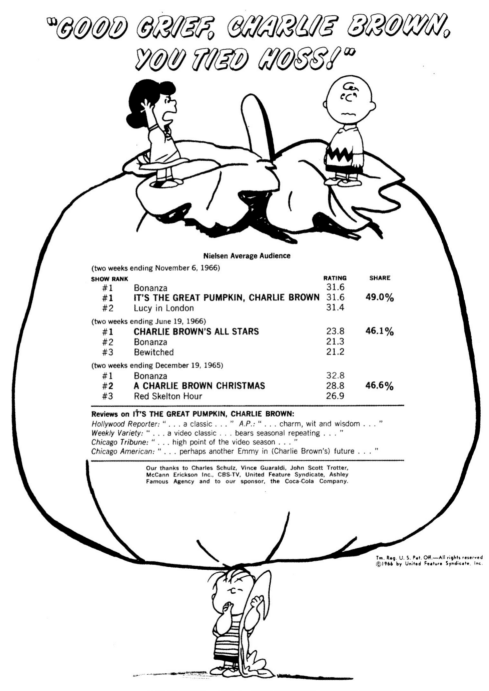

"GOOD GRIEF, CHARLIE BROWN, YOU TIED HOSS!"

Nielsen Average Audience

(two weeks ending November 6, 1966)

SHOW RANK		RATING	SHARE
#1	Bonanza	31.6	
#1	**IT'S THE GREAT PUMPKIN, CHARLIE BROWN**	31.6	49.0%
#2	Lucy in London	31.4	

(two weeks ending June 19, 1966)

#1	**CHARLIE BROWN'S ALL STARS**	23.8	46.1%
#2	Bonanza	21.3	
#3	Bewitched	21.2	

(two weeks ending December 19, 1965)

#1	Bonanza	32.8	
#2	**A CHARLIE BROWN CHRISTMAS**	28.8	46.6%
#3	Red Skelton Hour	26.9	

Reviews on IT'S THE GREAT PUMPKIN, CHARLIE BROWN:

Hollywood Reporter: " . . . a classic . . . " *A.P.:* " . . . charm, wit and wisdom . . . "
Weekly Variety: " . . . a video classic . . . bears seasonal repeating . . . "
Chicago Tribune: " . . . high point of the video season . . . "
Chicago American: " . . . perhaps another Emmy in (Charlie Brown's) future . . . "

Our thanks to Charles Schulz, Vince Guaraldi, John Scott Trotter, McCann Erickson Inc., CBS-TV, United Feature Syndicate, Ashley Famous Agency and to our sponsor, the Coca-Cola Company.

A LEE MENDELSON — BILL MELENDEZ PRODUCTION

> We have to do something different (pause). What if each time the kids go to get candy, Charlie Brown gets a rock?

Sparky laughed loudly. We all agreed it was a good idea.

> **Sparky:** And, yes, we can have a party. It can be very rough on Charlie Brown. We can do fun things that people have forgotten, like bobbing for apples. Maybe Lucy can bob and Snoopy can bob and they both come up with the same apple, or something like that. Or maybe she does the thing when she screams: "Arrrgh, I've been touched by dog lips." Anyway, we need a good party scene, with Vince's music.

When Sparky got going, the ideas would flow like water. The rest of that day and the next were spent integrating the different elements into the show. Sparky started writing the script, then Bill would storyboard what he had done and start the overall process.

That's how *It's the Great Pumpkin, Charlie Brown* evolved.

Was it the required blockbuster?

You bet! It was number one, tied with the ever-popular *Bonanza*. It had the highest rating of the top three specials—a 31.6 rating and 49 percent share of audience.

Over the years the critics have loved it too.

The Hollywood Reporter called it " . . . a classic . . . "

Associated Press raved that it had " . . . charm, wit, and wisdom . . . "

Weekly Variety dubbed it " . . . a video classic . . . bears repeating . . . "

Chicago Tribune acknowledged it as " . . . a high point of the video season . . . "

THE Hollywood REPORTER

Vol. CXCIII, No. 22   Hollywood, California, Tuesday, November 22, 1966   Price 10 Cents

LUCY BALL LOVES CHARLIE BROWN

RCA Oct. Color TV $ Sales Up 94% Over Last Year

New York. — RCA announced yesterday that October was the best color TV set sales month in its history in both dollars and units, with factory dollar sales up 94% over a year ago.

"The October record is especially significant since traditionally September is a stronger month than October for factory sales," according to Raymond W. Saxon, v-p and general manager, RCA Victor Home Instruments Division.

In addition to record color TV set sales, Saxon said unit sales for all RCA Victor home entertainment products—color and black-and-white TV sets, radios, phonographs and tape recorders—reached a new 10-month high mark this year. He did not give specific figures. He said RCA now is turning out more color sets than black-and-white units.

ABC Promotes Conley, Nettere

New York.—ABC, which last week announced widespread re-alignment in key executive personnel, continued its changes with announcements yesterday of new toppers in two areas.

Theodore F. Shaker, just named an ABC corporate group v-p, announced appointment of James E. Conley to succeed him as president of ABC-Owned TV Stations. Shaker also announced appointment of Fred L. Nettere to succeed Conley as president of ABC TV Spot Sales.

Conley and Nettere will report to Shaker who, in his new capacity as corporate group head reports to Simon B. Siegel, executive v-p of ABC, Inc., who is responsible for ABC-Owned TV Stations, ABC TV Spot Sales, ABC Films and ABC International.

Corman, UA to Film 'Judas' as Third Feature

Roger Corman Productions and United Artists have entered into an agreement to film "Judas" as the third film under their multiple non-exclusive association.

"Judas," which is being screenplayed by Sharon Compton from an idea by Corman, will follow "Robert E. Lee" and "The Spy In the Vatican" for Corman-UA.

Their Specials Take Top Nielsen; For First Time Movies Out Of Top Ten

It was pure TV in the latest Nielsens. For the first time this year, movies were not in the Top Ten. In fact they had slipped to the third frame of the Nielsens with regular and special TV shows taking higher position. Four specials — "It's a Great Pumpkin, Charlie Brown," "Lucy in London," "Ice Follies" and "Alice Through the Looking Glass" — dominated the Nielsen Top 10 for the two weeks ending Nov. 6, causing movies to slip down in the ratings chart with only two, the Tuesday Night Movie (23rd place) and the Sunday Night Movie (26th place), making the Top 30 where all five movie nights had made it in previous outings, two of them in the Top 10.

The only special of the period not scoring well was ABC's Tony Bennett show which made the bottom 15 with a surprisingly poor 11.6. Other specials scoring solidly included "Miss Teenage America" in 20th place with a 21.3 rating and National Geographic—
(Continued on Page 3)

NGP Buys Salinger Book on Kennedy

National General Productions, Inc., a subsidiary of National General Corp., has bought motion picture rights to Pierre Salinger's "With Kennedy," published by Doubleday & Co.

It also has been serialized in Good Housekeeping, been syndicated in U.S. newspapers, been sold for publication in nine foreign languages.

Salinger will assist in the writing of the screenplay and act as consultant on the film.

Mike Connolly Services At Blessed Sacrament

Funeral services for Mike Connolly, Hollywood Reporter columnist who died Friday, will be held today at 9 a.m. at Blessed Sacrament Church, 6657 Sunset Blvd., with a Requiem High Mass celebrated by Rev. James Roche. Rev. Willis Egan will deliver the eulogy.

Interment will follow in Holy Cross Cemetery, Culver City.

Music for the Mass will be performed by Paul Salamonovich, organist, and Brad Thomas soloist.

Gene Nelson to Direct 'Perils of Pauline' at U.

Gene Nelson set by producer Herbert B. Leonard to direct the forthcoming "Perils of Pauline," a Herbert B. Leonard Enterprises production for Universal release with Pat Boone and Pamela Austin starring.

Nelson checks in at Universal today to complete preparations on the picture which is scheduled to go before the Technicolor cameras on Nov. 29.

UA's Merger With Trans-America Latest In Corporate Maneuvers

New York. — Merger of United Artists with Transamerica Corp. of San Francisco represents the latest in a series of corporate maneuvers involving Hollywood film companies, as stockholders or company directors work to give the studios a more favorable financial position. The key word is "diversify."

Transamerica's absorption of UA as a wholly owned subsidiary is similar to Gulf & Western's takeover of Paramount some weeks earlier. The Transamerica-UA merger was managed with a tax-free exchange of shares, and announced late Sunday by UA board chairman Robert S. Benjamin and president Arthur B. Krim, and by Transamerica president John R. Beckett.

The announcement stressed there would be no change of policies on the part of UA, and the present management would continue in office. The merger is subject to stockholder approval, but this is believed a formality.

In a way, the change is linked, too, with Jack L. Warner's sale of his 1,600,000 shares in Warners to Seven Arts. By giving the various companies as broad a base as possible in divergent economic interests, the companies are considered sounder financially under current tax laws, allowing write-
(Continued on Page 4)

AFTRA, Mediator Fail to Disclose Settlement Pact

New York. — The tentative agreement of the American Federation of Television and Radio Artists with the networks covers for the first time all national newsmen rendering service for on-the-air broadcasts, Donald F. Conaway, the talent union's national executive secretary, told The Hollywood Reporter yesterday. However, Conaway declined, as did network labor relations representatives and Federal Mediator Abraham A. Desser, to disclose any details of the settlement reached Sunday night. All said there was a gentlemen's agreement not to discuss the provisions.

Negotiated pacts will be presented for approval to the western section of the AFTRA board Monday by Conaway. The proposed contracts were submitted by him to the eastern board members late yesterday. The Chicago portion of the board will pass on the new codes Nov. 30. These codes cover national TV, commercial and sustaining radio, transcriptions, tape commercials and network newsmen.

The newsmen provisions encompass services, duties, rates of pay and working conditions. They embrace commen-
(Continued on Page 4)

'Gambit' Preems Dec. 21

"Gambit," Universal's Christmas release, will world premiere Dec. 21 at New York's Sutton Theatre, it was announced by Henry H. "Hi" Martin, Universal v-p and general sales manager. The Technicolor romantic suspense comedy, starring Shirley MacLaine and Michael Caine, opens an exclusive first run locally Dec. 23 at the Village Theatre in Westwood.

Cooper Dimes Chairman

Jackie Cooper has been reappointed California Chairman for 1967 March of Dimes it was announced by Basil O'Connor, president of The National Foundation-March of Dimes. The Campaign for funds to support this voluntary health agency in its fight against birth defects is held in January.

'Zhivago' Matinees

MGM's "Doctor Zhivago," now in its 48th week at the Hollywood Paramount Theatre, will have a two-a-day matinee and evening performance schedule beginning with the Saturday matinee, Dec. 17 through Monday, Jan. 2.

October 27, 1966 **Thursday**
Evening

Guest Cast
Princess Little Fawn ....Brenda Benét
Stinch ....Laurie Main
5 COLOR **TRUTH OR CONSE-QUENCES—Game**
7 **8** **BATMAN—Adventure**
COLOR "The Dead Ringers," conclusion. Super-criminal Chandell (alias Fingers) is wooing Aunt Harriet in an attempt to get his hands on the Wayne fortune. Batman: Adam West. Robin: Burt Ward. Aunt Harriet: Madge Blake. Gordon: Neil Hamilton. O'Hara: Stafford Repp. Alfred: Alan Napier.
Guest Cast
Chandell ....Liberace
Alfred Slye ....James Millhollin
Doe ....Marilyn Hanold
9 **MOVIE—Western**
Million Dollar Movie: "Run for Cover." See Mon. 7:30 P.M. Ch. 9 for details.
11 **HONEYMOONERS—Comedy**
Ralph receives a summons from the Bureau of Internal Revenue. Ralph: Jackie Gleason. Norton: Art Carney.

13 **INTERNATIONAL MAGAZINE**
SPECIAL Reports: 1. Social attitudes toward unwed mothers in the U.S., Sweden and Britain; 2. Nationalism in Aden, the British protectorate on the tip of the Arabian Peninsula; 3. A visit to Norfolk, England, home of Abraham Lincoln's ancestors; and 4. A profile of Philibert Tsiranana, President of the Malagasy Republic. (60 min.)
31 **ON THE JOB—Fire Dept.**
47 **CARLOTA Y MAXIMILIANO**
8:00 **3** **MR. ROBERTS—Comedy**
COLOR A pretty lady lieutenant comes aboard ship requesting medical supplies. Lilli: Joan Freeman.
5 **MY FAVORITE MARTIAN**
Uncle Martin gives Tim the power to read minds—for one day only. Tim: Bill Bixby. Martin: Ray Walston.
7 **8** **F TROOP—Comedy**
COLOR Derby Dan McGurney, candidate in a tied election for mayor of Corporal Agarn's home town, carries his campaign to the Fort—and to his constit-

Thursday October 27, 1966
Evening

uent, whose absentee ballot can break the deadlock. Agarn: Larry Storch. O'Rourke: Forrest Tucker. Parmenter: Ken Berry. Wrangler Jane: Melody Patterson. Wild Eagle: Frank de Kova.
Guest Cast
Derby Dan McGurney ....Tol Avery
Mindy ....Luana Patten
George Bragan ....Lew Parker
11 **MUNSTERS—Comedy**
Igor the bat, Eddie's entry in the school pet fair, has flown the coop—so Grandpa agrees to take its place. Herman: Fred Gwynne. Lily: Yvonne DeCarlo. Eddie: Butch Patrick. Grandpa: Al Lewis.
31 **LATIN AMERICA—Education**
"Spain and Portugal: Pioneers of European Expansion." Dr. Peterson.
47 **REVISTA DEL HOGAR**
8:30 **2** **3** **CHARLIE BROWN**
SPECIAL COLOR "It's the Great Pumpkin, Charlie Brown." See the Close-up on page A-83. (60 min.)
"My Three Sons" is pre-empted.

4 **STAR TREK—Adventure**
COLOR "Miri." The Enterprise responds to a distress call from a planet that is the exact duplicate of earth as it was in the 1960's—except that it is populated only by strange, wild children. Script by Adrian Spies. Kirk: William Shatner. Spock: Leonard Nimoy. McCoy: DeForest Kelley. Janice: Grace Lee Whitney. Farrell: Jim Goodwin. (60 min.)
Guest Cast
Miri ....Kim Darby
Jahn ....Michael J. Pollard
Fat Little Boy ....John Megna
5 **BRANDED—Western**
COLOR McCord, stricken by diptheria, risks his life to test a serum. McCord: Chuck Connors. Dr. Karen Miller: Patricia Medina. Newt Woolery: Michael Forest. Mark: Johnny Crawford.
7 **8** COLOR **DATING GAME**
11 **HONEY WEST—Mystery**
Honey investigates the murder of a private detective who was blown up in his car. Honey: Anne Francis. Garth: Steve Ihnat. Charlie: Harry Bellaver.

TV CLOSE-UP GUIDE
8:30 **2** **3** **CHARLIE BROWN—Cartoon**

'It's the Great Pumpkin, Charlie Brown'

SPECIAL COLOR This Halloween cartoon features Charlie and his pals from Charles Schulz' "Peanuts" comic strip.
The Halloween season means happiness for Charlie Brown, who has finally been invited to a party; heroics for Snoopy, the canine combatant, who plans to go aloft after the Red Baron; and the moment of truth for Linus, who awaits the arrival of the Great Pumpkin "with his bag of toys for all the good children."
Bill Melendez Associates animated Schulz' story. Music by Vince Guaraldi, arranged by John Scott Trotter.
Voices . . . Charlie Brown: Peter Robbins. Linus: Chris Shea. Lucy: Sally Dryer. Sally: Kathy Steinberg. Patty: Lisa DeFaria. Frieda: Ann Altieri.

Charlie, Linus and the Great Pumpkin

GHOULIES AND GHOSTIES AND LONG-LEGGED BEASTIES AND THINGS THAT GO BUMP IN THE NIGHT NEVER WERE BETTER TELEVISION THAN THEY ARE ON "IT'S THE GREAT PUMPKIN, CHARLIE BROWN!" BROUGHT TO YOU BY THE PEOPLE IN YOUR TOWN WHO BOTTLE COCA-COLA. DON'T MISS IT. AND DON'T TELL US YOU'RE TOO OLD TO BELIEVE IN GREAT PUMPKINS.

See "It's The Great Pumpkin, Charlie Brown!" Thurs., 8:30 p.m., Ch 2-3.
© UNITED FEATURES SYNDICATE, INC. 1950 ALL RIGHTS RESERVED
"COCA-COLA" AND "COKE" ARE REGISTERED TRADE-MARKS WHICH IDENTIFY ONLY THE PRODUCT OF THE COCA-COLA COMPANY.

TV GUIDE   A-83   A-84   TV GUIDE

And so on.

In *The Hollywood Reporter*, the front-page headline screamed: Lucy Ball Loves Charlie Brown, and they wrote:

"For the first time this year, movies were not in the Top Ten . . . . Four specials . . . dominated the Nielsens Top 10 . . . [topped by] 'It's the Great Pumpkin, Charlie Brown' at Number One."

So CBS had its blockbuster after all . . . they ordered four more shows . . . and Sparky, Bill, and I would go on to eventually create 50 prime time network specials during 38 years. None of which would have happened if *Pumpkin* hadn't been so successful. So that was our gift from Santa Claus—excuse me, the Great Pumpkin—in the fall of 1966.

THE ACTORS

Believe it or not, from 1963–1965—prior to the success of our network specials—I had been unable to sell a *Peanuts* special to the television honchos for one reason only: the executives would say, "How can you have kids speaking the kinds of thoughts and words we expect to hear from adults? It won't sound natural." They would ask this even though Bill Melendez and Sparky Schulz had used children's voices in all the animated Ford commercials that featured *Peanuts* characters back in 1960 . . . and even though Bill and I did the same thing for a documentary about Schulz in 1963 . . . and even though *Peanuts* was already a world-famous comic strip by 1963!

They also wondered how we would pick the right voices when everyone who reads the comic strip had their own idea about how the characters should sound. And they weren't sure why we would use children's voices when adults always did

FOR YOUR CONSIDERATION AS EMMY NOMINEE FOR BEST ACTOR OF THE YEAR*

*"IT'S THE GREAT PUMPKIN, CHARLIE BROWN!"

THIS THURSDAY NIGHT (OCT. 27) CBS-TV 8:30-9:00

After "Charlie Brown's All Stars," many critics nominated Snoopy for an Emmy for best supporting actor. But his upcoming, co-starring performance as the World War I Flying Ace chasing the Red Baron in "It's the Great Pumpkin, Charlie Brown!", surpasses even his earlier triumphs. Good grief!

Our thanks to Coca-Cola, McCann Erickson, Charles Schulz, and United Feature Syndicate for making all this possible.

LEE MENDELSON-BILL MELENDEZ

the kids' voices in cartoons anyway?

Of course this seems like such nonsense now, but that's what I encountered for two years.

Then in April 1965, *Time* magazine put the *Peanuts* characters on its cover. Suddenly, qualms about the "voices" for *Peanuts* disappeared as far as TV executives were concerned. Coca-Cola bought *A Charlie Brown Christmas* and we were on our way.

We had originally thought that we would do just one *Peanuts* special and that would be that. But now we were suddenly faced with the challenge of doing many specials. Since the voices of the young children we would cast would change every two years, we realized we would need to recast the characters just as frequently. Typically the age of the actors was between six and seven years for Marcie and Sally and between nine and eleven for Charlie Brown, Linus, and Lucy.

We decided two things: First, we would keep each actor as long as possible, and second, when we did get new voices they would have to match the voices of the original Christmas cast. The voices of Snoopy and Woodstock

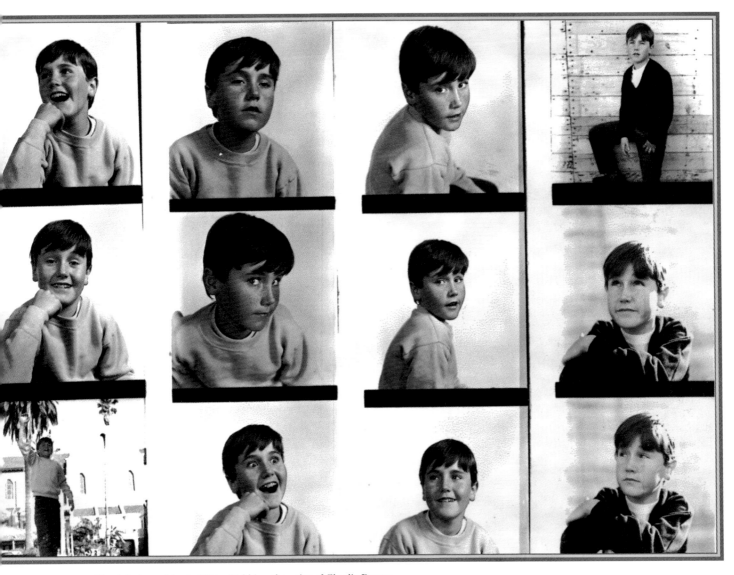

Head shot proofsheet of Peter Robbins, the voice of Charlie Brown

would be no problem as Bill Melendez had recorded those by speaking gibberish and then speeding up the recording. Those have never changed to this day.

I called Peter Robbins and Chris Shea, who played Charlie Brown and Linus on the Christmas show, and I was thrilled to discover that their voices had not

Peter Robbins

Peter Robbins

changed, so they were signed for the Pumpkin show immediately. The part of Charlie Brown is very difficult for an actor. He has to be a good actor, of course, but he has to do it with that blah "Charlie Brown voice." That's quite a chore for a ten year old; Peter pulled it off in every show he recorded.

I recently met with Peter and Bill Melendez in Bill's studio. Peter said he remembers being fascinated by Bill's very active mustache.

"No matter how many shows we did," said Peter, "we always looked forward to watching Bill perform."

From left to right: Lee Mendelson, Peter Robbins, and Bill Melendez in 2005

I asked Peter what he most remembered about the *Great Pumpkin* recording back in the spring of 1966.

"Well, first of all, I couldn't understand why I was the only one getting a rock in my trick or treat bag. All the other kids thought it was very funny, but I sure didn't. I had never heard of such a thing happening to anybody on Halloween.

"But the most confusing thing to me—and to all the kids—was all this talk about 'The Great Pumpkin.' Naturally none of us had heard of anything being called that before. It kind of spooked us out.

"And then we watched and listened as Linus and Sally had their yelling and screaming bout in the Pumpkin Patch, and so we were even more confused. I must admit . . . nothing made sense to us . . . but we were having fun doing it anyway."

Chris Shea, the voice of Linus

I've heard from many critics and viewers during the past four decades—and I must agree—that the performances of Chris Shea as Linus reading so beautifully from the Bible in *A Charlie Brown Christmas* and then screaming from the Pumpkin Patch in *Great Pumpkin* are two of the most memorable scenes in animated television history. Chris goes back in *Peanuts* history even further than I do. Five years before the Christmas and Pumpkin shows, Bill Melendez animated a commercial for the new Ford Falcon, the first time *Peanuts* had ever been animated. A very young Chris was the voice of Linus in that commercial.

"At that time, I remember feeling very close to the character of Linus. In fact when I was questioned by a magazine about it, I recall telling them that I liked playing Linus because he was kind of a philosopher, and I felt that way too."

I recently spoke with Chris and this is what he said about his experiences:

"When I first started playing the voice of Linus I was very young—five years old, I believe—and then we made *Charlie Brown's All Stars!* very quickly. But I really got excited when we started work on *The Great Pumpkin*. I had very few lines in *All Stars* but I was very excited to see that I had a whole bunch of lines in *Pumpkin*. And it was so much fun to do all those scenes with Sally in the Pumpkin Patch.

"At that time, I remember feeling very close to the character of Linus. In fact when I was questioned by a magazine about it, I recall telling them that I liked playing Linus because he was kind of a philosopher, and I felt that way too.

"Working with Bill Melendez was one of the great joys for me and the other kids. We loved his big mustache. When he would do the voice of Snoopy, he would throw his head back and howl at the moon. I loved watching his mustache quiver. Then, to create the final voice of Snoopy, they would speed up the sound.

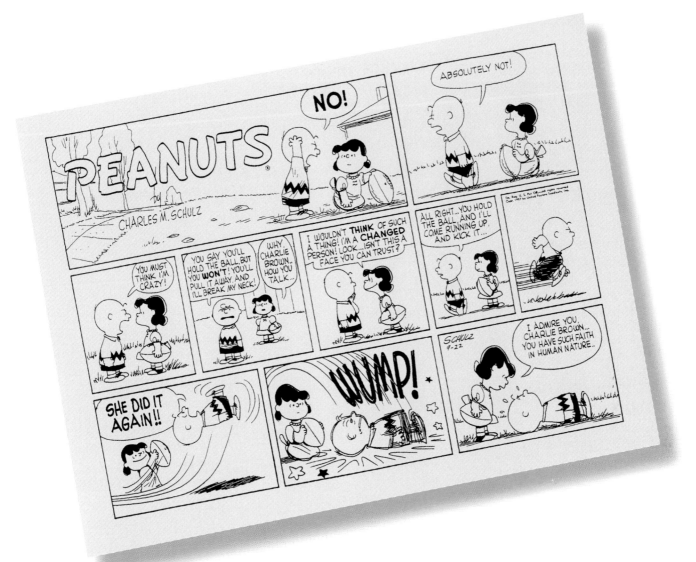

"Bill's patience and exuberance was another thing that greatly endeared him to us. I remember one time sitting at the table across from him as we were reading our lines for *Pumpkin*. I was a very enthusiastic child, bordering on hyper, and I took advantage of all the perks—especially the soda machine. The more soda I drank, the more I tapped my foot. I know it was frustrating to Bill, but he calmly said that we would record again and he patiently asked me to please stop tapping, which I did. He really knew how to handle us!"

At the audition for Lucy, we were pleased to find out that Sally Dreyer, who had smaller parts on our first two shows, had grown into a perfect Lucy voice.

When I spoke with her recently in her Arizona home she shared the following:

"I was thrilled when I was promoted from Violet in the Christmas show to Lucy in *Charlie Brown's All Stars!* and then *The Great Pumpkin*. I remember I had mixed feelings about the lines I had to deliver in *Pumpkin*. On the one hand, it was fun to be the crabby Lucy. On the other hand, I didn't like being mean to Charlie Brown."

"One worry that all the kids had at the time was when our voices might change, because we noticed new people would come on to the show. Fortunately, I was able to do four more shows as Lucy after *Pumpkin*. It's funny even today that people get very excited when they hear I was Lucy. So thirty-nine years of fame beats fifteen minutes!"

Sally Dryer, the voice of Lucy

One of the favorite characters early on in *Peanuts* was Frieda. She thought she was better than anyone else because of her hair. She was actually very pompous about it. Anne Altieri, the daughter of one of my closest friends, not only had naturally curly hair like Frieda but she also had the perfect voice for that character as well as the character Violet, whom she also played in *It's the Great Pumpkin Charlie Brown.* We often taped half of our shows in Hollywood, using professional actors, and half in San Francisco, where we found unusual voices who were not necessarily professional actors. Anne was, of course, one of the latter.

When we met recently she shared some of her memories of the making of the show—and she still had that great hair, nearly 40 years later!

"One thing I remember from our recording sessions is that I would always throw up on the way home. I was kind of a shy girl, so I guess it was kind of stressful on me.

"Parts of my real life were so small at that time, when I got to be Violet and got to invite everyone to my house for the Halloween party, that was a big deal for me. And then to have the lines about drawing on the back of

Anne Altieri, the voice of Freida, with Bill Melendez

Charlie Brown's head—that was really exciting for a little, shy kid.

"It's funny, when I listen to the show now I don't recognize my voice at all, but I remember *every* feeling I had about every line I delivered thirty-nine years ago! It's all like a magnificent dream."

We needed a very strong actress for Sally, and we found one in six-year-old Cathy Steinberg. She carried the very difficult scenes in the Pumpkin Patch when she became so frustrated with Linus.

Sisters Lisa and Gabrielle DeFaria (Ritter) were daughters of my partner, Walt DeFaria, and played Pigpen and Patty respectively on *Great Pumpkin*. Gabrielle recalls this about our San Francisco recording sessions on *Pumpkin*:

"I remember the first time we went to record in San Francisco. Bill would feed us one line at a time. When we had breaks, we ran all around the studio to blow off steam. Vince Guaraldi would often be recording next door. When the musicians took their breaks, we would run in and play the piano. We made up a song: 'Vince Guaraldi . . . he's a baldy.' We thought it was funny because we thought it rhymed. Vince caught us once and we were scared we would get into trouble, but he just laughed.

"We always wondered why both Vince and Bill

Anne Altieri with Lee Mendelson, 2005

had these big handlebar mustaches. One was unusual but two was overwhelming at times.

"One time, a musical group from next door came in and asked for our autographs. We had no idea who they were or why they wanted our signatures. Turns out they were the Jefferson Airplane!

"Another special moment occurred when we were posing for *TV Guide*. That was really exciting!

"We felt very special when we did the recordings. And it's been extra special that people have enjoyed the shows for forty years."

A few years later, when Peppermint Patty came along in the comic strip and into our TV shows, we were trying to figure out what kind of voice to give her. We were at the Hippo Restaurant in San Francisco, which was famous for their hamburgers. Gabrielle DeFaria yelled: "Please pass the mustard!!" in a very deep guttural voice, which she recalls as being a cross between a line backer and a sports announcer.

Lisa DeFaria, the voice of Pigpen

Her dad and I looked at each other with the same thought. I ran to the pay phone, called Bill Melendez at home, and said, "We just found the perfect voice for Peppermint Patty." In fact, all three of the DeFaria siblings—Lisa, Gabrielle, and their brother Chris, who is now a great producer at Warner Bros.—would play Peppermint Patty at different times. Gabrielle says her son has the exact same voice. Good genes are good genes!

My son Glenn, then nine, now fifty, also had one line as Schroeder, but it was a great one. After the kids agree to bob for apples, Schroeder says, "Yeah, Lucy, you should be good at this. You have the perfect mouth for it." That was the beginning and the end of Glenn's acting career, but it served him well. Now he's copresident of our company.

I didn't use my children often but each had at least one shot. My daughter Lynda did a few shows. My son Sean had one line on our

Gabrielle DeFaria, voice of Patty

show about the Mayflower voyage: "I think I'm going to throw up!" The only "star" was my son Jason. He did the original Re-Run voice at age five, and then went on to do Marcie and Peppermint Patty in many of the shows. I myself had one line, "Strike three," in *All Stars*.

I always felt that the cast for *Pumpkin* was by far one of the best we ever had. We have had more than 150 actors in the various casts during 38 years of production. One of our Sallys was Stacy Ferguson—now starring with the group Black Eyed Peas. She was a great singer even then when she was only eight!!

"The hardest thing Bill Melendez and I had to do throughout the years was to tell one of our major actors that his or her voice had gotten too old for the part."

The hardest thing Bill Melendez and I had to do throughout the years was to tell one of our major actors that his or her voice had gotten too old for the part.

On the fortunate side, many of our crabby Sallys would grow into the crabby Lucy parts. Many of the "hoarse-sounding" Marcies would grow into the Peppermint Pattys. Three Shea brothers would play Linus during ten years. The aforementioned DeFarias were Peppermint Patty for nearly eight years.

A while back, we invited all the actors together for a special lunch. Roughly 65 of them were able to attend. Most of them of course came with their own young children and babies. It was quite a thrill to see so many of them again in one room. The simple fact is that they saved us every time. They were the key to making each show a success. We will never forget them!

VINCE GUARALDI AND THE GREAT PUMPKIN

Vince Guaraldi was at home alone, working on the musical score of *Great Pumpkin* one evening. His family was away on a short trip. After taking a shower he wrapped a towel around himself.

It was around 2 AM and he heard strange noises in his front yard. As the noises grew louder and more ominous, he went to the door and opened it slightly. He couldn't see anything, but the noises persisted. He ventured farther out the door, failing to notice that his towel had dropped off. At the same time he lost his grip on the front door handle and it slammed shut. Whatever noises he had heard earlier had stopped, but now the front door was locked. He was left standing out there in the buff! How would he get back into the house?

Vince Guaraldi

He looked up at the second story window and saw that it was slightly ajar. He ran naked to the garage and got a ladder that would reach upstairs. Now, Vince would be the first one to admit that he didn't have a build like Brad Pitt. He was short and stubby, "kind of round," he often said of himself. When he was halfway up the ladder, a police car pulled up.

The policeman got out of the car, flashed a spotlight on the naked composer, and shouted, "What's the deal? Who are you?"

And Vince, without missing a beat, yelled down, "Don't shoot . . . I'm the Great Pumpkin." True story!

Despite his bum luck at 2 AM, Vince eventually finished the score, and it was fantastic. He had three shows under his belt by then: the documentary, *Christmas*, and *All Stars*. How he created the music for *Pumpkin* pretty much tells the story of how he created the music for all 16 *Peanuts* specials that he worked on before his untimely passing. *Pumpkin*, as fans will recall, has a myriad of scenes and changes of mood. As a result, Vince liked to come up with as many different music cuts as possible. He wrote 20 original songs for the show, including "The Red Baron" and the oft recorded "Great Pumpkin Waltz." He even expanded his trio into a sextet that included a plaintiff flute—perfect for the loneliness of Linus in the pumpkin patch.

Although his song "Linus and Lucy" had been a big hit in the Christmas special, it was hardly known outside of the show.

Vince thought we should make "Linus and Lucy" a major theme of the *Pumpkin* show as well, so the first two minutes of the show feature Linus and Lucy pantomiming while Vince's group is blasting the song away. This was unique for a cartoon. Now, of course, the song is recognized by all. One can rarely go to a store during the Christmas season without hearing it.

Vince also knew when *not* to have music. As noted earlier, the first time we animated Snoopy was during the Flying Ace sequence in *Pumpkin*. Vince said the scene did not require any music, and he was right. Sound effects did the trick instead.

Another equally important "first" on this show was how we animated one of the most famous scenes ever in the *Peanuts* comic strip—a scene that has been repeated in many of our TV shows. The famous first I'm referring to is the one where Lucy pulls the football away from Charlie Brown. We all wondered what could accompany the scene, but Vince said, "There shouldn't be any music here at all. The dialogue and action are great by themselves." Vince also suggested that we not have music over the climactic scene with Sally and Linus in the Pumpkin Patch, and he was right again. The two young actors—Cathy Steinberg and Chris Shea—carried the day!

Another memorable musical moment that

Vince contributed to the show concerns Schroeder and his toy piano, which Sparky had always liked to include in every special. Since we had the WWI Flying Ace on the show, Sparky suggested that we have Snoopy dance to some WWI songs. Bill Melendez created one of our most talked about animated scenes as Vince played his real piano (as if it were a toy piano) to "It's a Long Way to Tipperary" and three other WWI classics.

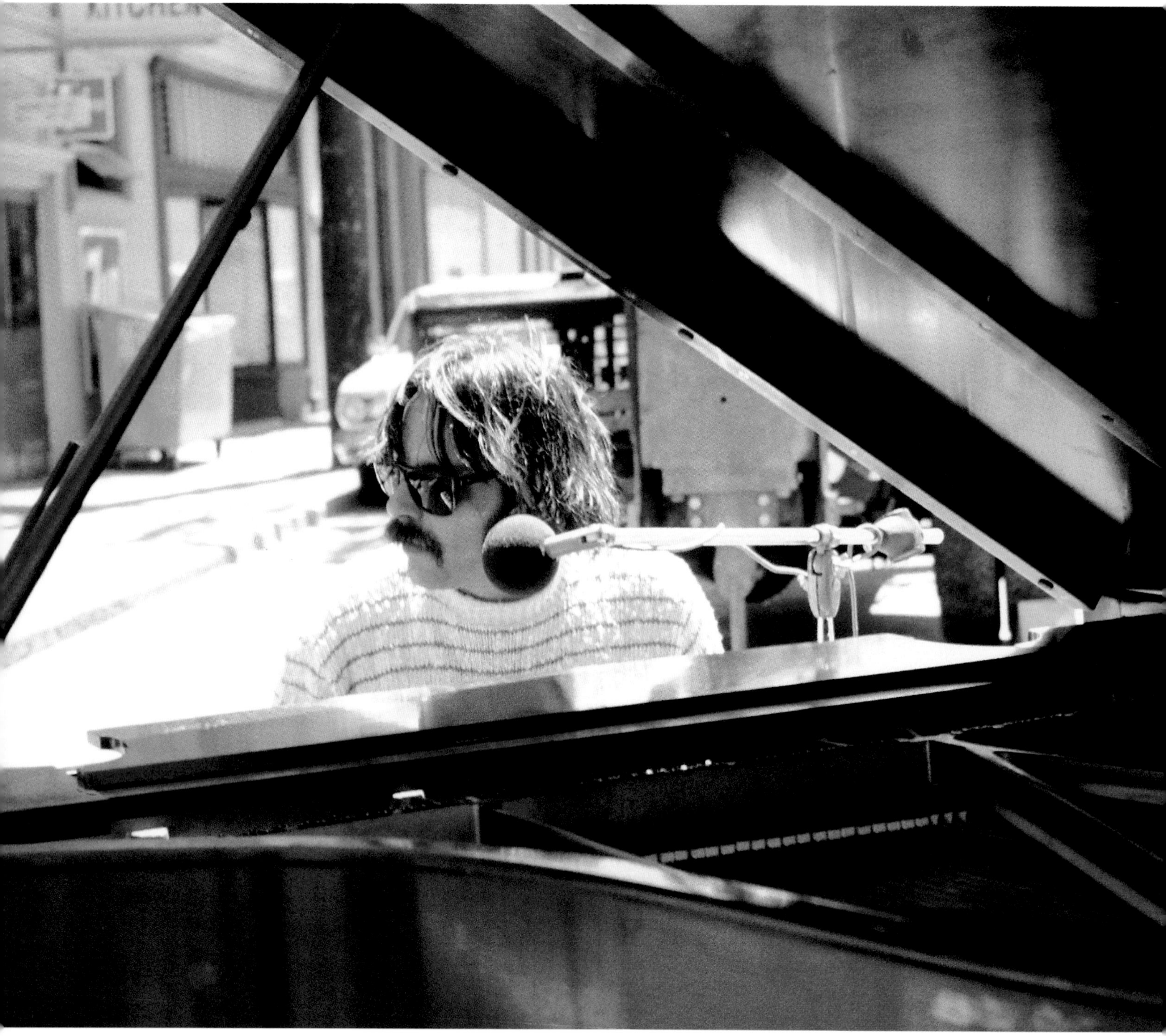

Vince Guaraldi

The next time you watch *Pumpkin*, see and hear how important the music is to the show. Perhaps the question I am most asked is why we picked jazz in the first place, since it had never been associated with animation before.

TV Guide conducted an online poll not too long ago that was answered by 3,700 people. It asked this question: "Which musical moment from the '60s rocked TV the most?"

First place went to the Beatles, of course, but Vince Guaraldi's score for *A Charlie Brown Christmas* took second place. Now the first recordings I ever remember hearing in our San Francisco flat in the late 1930s and early 1940s were my dad's 78s of musicians such as Art Tatum, Duke Ellington, and Count Basie. My father was a devotee of jazz. There was something about the genre in the later days of the Great Depression and World War II, especially, that somehow "kept hope alive." And those old 78s never left me! I've always been a jazz fan.

In 1963 when I was doing the documentary on Charles Schulz I remember listening to the local jazz station while driving over the Golden Gate Bridge. I was trying to figure out what kind of music we should use. At that moment I heard Vince's "Cast Your Fate to the Wind," a Grammy-winning song as it turned out. When I discovered that he lived in San Francisco I sought him out and signed him to do the music for the documentary. Vince's label was called Fantasy Records. He actually recorded the music in a basement on Treat Street in San Francisco.

An interesting side note: Within a few months in 1963, Vince and the Beatles were both recording; Vince for us and the Beatles in England. Just six years later in

> "The next time you watch Pumpkin, see and hear how important the music is to the show."

1969, two of the Oscar nominees for best Original Score were the Beatles for "Let It Be" and Vince for our first Charlie Brown feature film.

In those days the nominees attended a pre-Oscar dinner. We found ourselves at the same table as Paul McCartney. This was a brief moment in our conversation:

McCartney: (totally serious) Well, we all know who's going to win. Charlie Brown! And I really mean that.

Lee: (in total disbelief) You can't be serious. No one can beat you guys.

McCartney: It's a sure thing . . . Charlie Brown!

Unfortunately, I was right, and "Let It Be" won the Oscar. But it's amazing to me how far two "garage bands" (ours was a basement band, too) had come between 1963 and 1969.

The first song Vince wrote blew me away. He called it "Linus and Lucy," and the rest is history as far as that song is concerned. In addition to "Linus and Lucy" Vince also recorded eight other tunes for the documentary we were doing on Schulz.

Fantasy Records had planned to release about 5,000 albums featuring these songs. We had an equal number of 8 x 10 color pictures of the *Peanuts* characters, and four of us stuffed them into the albums. One of these "stuffers" from Fantasy was a man named Saul Zaentz. Years later, while watching the Oscars, I almost passed out as the same Saul Zaentz picked up his Oscar for producing "One Flew Over the Cuckoo's Nest."

> "The first song Vince wrote blew me away. He called it "Linus and Lucy," and the rest is history as far as that song is concerned."

Unfortunately we never sold the documentary, and the album did just moderately well. But two years later—when we were planning the Christmas show and then the Pumpkin show—Sparky, Bill, and I remembered Vince's trio from that San Francisco basement. We called him and thankfully he was interested in working with us on the specials. That's how jazz became a part of the *Peanuts* TV world.

Jazz pianist David Benoit—who has done the scores for 20 of our *Peanuts* specials since the untimely passing of Vince Guaraldi—also told me the reason he started playing the piano was because, as a child, he was inspired by Vince's music on *Peanuts*. He clearly knew the sound we were looking for and so the transition from Vince's performance of the music to David's was quite natural.

The talented George Winston did the score for one of our *Peanuts* shows in the miniseries *This is America, Charlie Brown*. His album of Guaraldi tunes sold more than 800,000 copies. He also credits hearing the *Peanuts* music as a child with inspiring him to enter the music field.

We've also been lucky to have Wynton Marsalis score one of our *Peanuts* history shows entitled *The Wright Brothers at Kitty Hawk*. He too has a successful album combining some Guaraldi *Peanuts* music with some of his own music. He wrote in the album notes for *Joe Cool's Blues*:

When I was a boy, the only time you would hear jazz on television was when Charlie Brown came to town. I always liked the feeling that the music put on the cartoon. Sometimes I read the comic strip and I loved the fact that Charlie Brown was always trying, even though he inevitably met with failure or that special kind of humiliation that was roundly cheered by his friends. For me, it was a combination because I didn't

> "There were many reasons for the success of the Peanuts television specials, which critics have often called a seamless transition from the comic page."

think of the comic strip on the page apart from the television cartoon and Vince Guaraldi's music, which I liked because it was happy and upbeat.

There were many reasons for the success of the *Peanuts* television specials, which critics have often called a seamless transition from the comic page to the television screen. Vince's music was one of the key ingredients. I think it's because the music appeals to both adults and children, and that's a rare combination. Sparky, who loved all kinds of music, was immediately taken by "Linus and Lucy" when he first heard it back in 1963, as were Bill Melendez and I. The Guaraldi music will always be associated with *Peanuts*, and future generations will love it for decades to come.

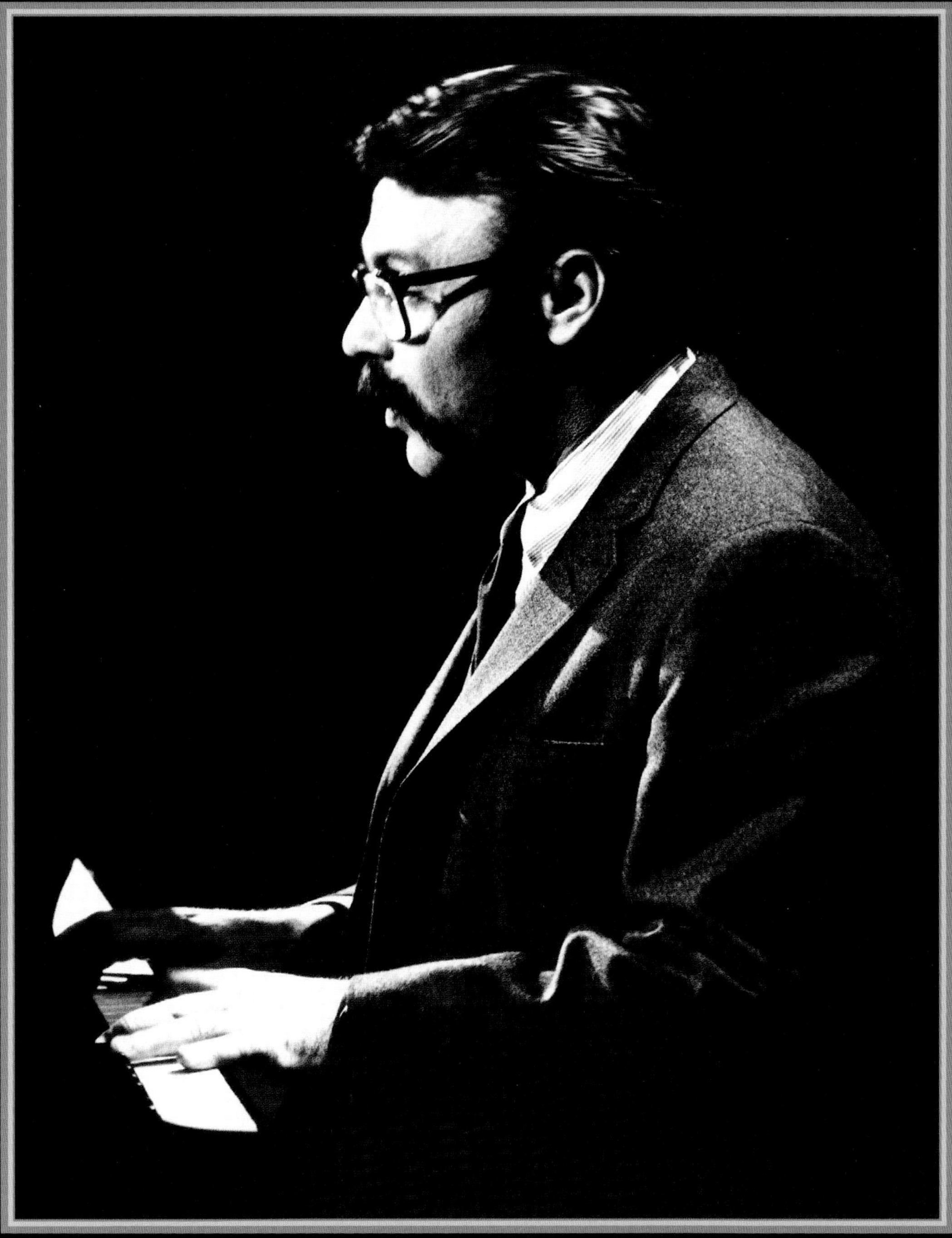

Vince Guaraldi

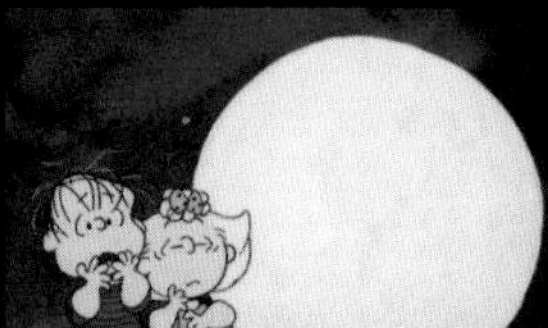

BILL MELENDEZ: ANIMATOR EXTRAORDINAIRE

Charles Schulz was so impressed by the way Bill Melendez first animated the *Peanuts* characters in the Ford commercials they created together—by simply drawing the characters as they appeared in the comic strip and moving them with no "Hollywood embellishments"—that he decided Bill Melendez would be the only animator to ever do it again in the future. And that "promise" lasted for four decades. Bill and I first met in 1963, when he animated two minutes of *Peanuts* for the documentary I was making of Charles Schulz. Since then, our logo "A Lee Mendelson–Bill Melendez Production" has appeared on 50 prime-time animated specials—the most in television history!

Together we produced eighteen Charlie Brown and Snoopy shows for Saturday morning television and four animated feature films: *Snoopy Come Home*; *Race for Your Life, Charlie Brown*; *Bon Voyage, Charlie Brown*; and *A Boy Named Charlie Brown*, which received an Oscar nomination for Original Score.

We have also been the lucky and proud recipients of five Emmys and fifteen Emmy nominations, as well as two Peabody Awards for our work on *Peanuts*. Our most recent special, *He's a Bully, Charlie Brown*, airing in 2006, will mark 43 years together as creative partners. I've been fortunate to work with the best in the business—in addition to the work we did with *Peanuts*, Bill's credits include some of the great Disney pictures like *Dumbo*, *Pinocchio*, *Fantasia*, and *Bambi*, and he has won more than a dozen national and international awards for his animation.

We've also had the pleasure of working together on a number of other projects, including the first two *Garfield* specials, three

Lee Mendelson and Bill Melendez posing with the Emmy for Best Network Animated Special in 1966 for *A Charlie Brown Christmas*

Cathy specials—including an Emmy Award–winner, and two one-hour specials on the greatest comic strips of the past 100 years. But I think he and I both feel that *The Great Pumpkin* was one of his greatest achievements.

After the passing of Sparky in 2000, the Schulz

Lee Mendelson and Bill Melendez in 2005 with the five Emmys received for their work on *Peanuts*

family was kind enough to let us continue production of five more specials based on stories that we had already outlined with Sparky or stories he had developed in the comic strip itself. Though working on them without Schulz was difficult, Bill and I had our friendship and long work history to see us through. Nearing his eighty-ninth birthday, Bill's son Steve interviewed him, about the animation for *The Great Pumpkin* special. Here's how that conversation went:

Steve: How did you become the "voice" of Snoopy, which was part of this show?

Bill: Well, I had brought in an actor to be the voice. I told the actor what I wanted him to do. We tried many times and, for some reason, he just couldn't get it. Finally, the engineer called me out of the room and said: "Bill, you do it perfectly. Why don't *you* do it yourself." So that's how I became the voice of Snoopy for the next thirty-eight years. Just by accident.

A funny thing happened a few years ago. I was in a minor car accident and a policeman came by to get all the information. He kept looking at me. Suddenly he said: "Hey, you're the voice of Snoopy." It turned out he knew just about everything about *Peanuts*.

Steve: At the top of *It's the Great Pumpkin, Charlie Brown*, Snoopy was on all fours. That's the only time I remember seeing him that way.

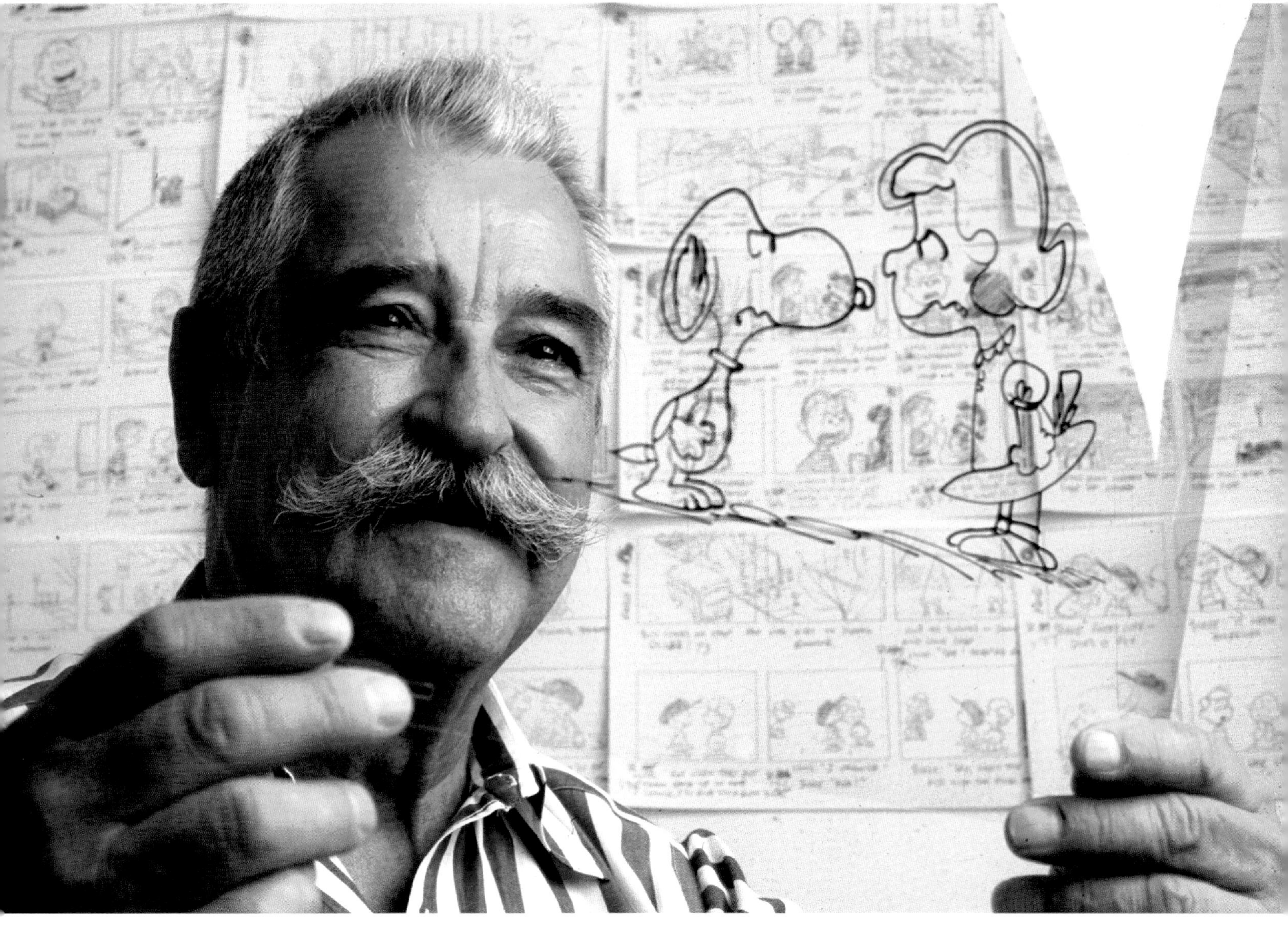

Bill Melendez circa 1985

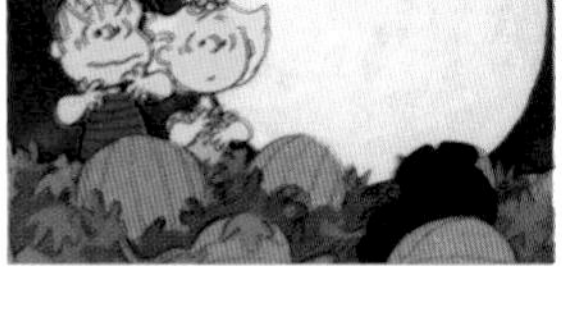

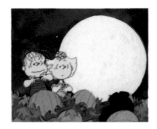

Bill: Well, Snoopy was on all fours in some of the early strips and, for some reason, we had him on all fours in this scene when Charlie Brown is raking leaves. But after that, we realized he just had to stand on his two feet to make it more cartoony.

Steve: And was the whole flying sequence for Snoopy created by you?

Bill: Sparky got very excited when I showed him how Snoopy could actually fly.

Steve: There was that funny thing with his fists, with the pumping action on the machine gun.

Bill: All I was doing was interpreting what I had seen in motion pictures of WWI scenes, and then of course we added the sound effects, which really made the scene come alive. This was one of the best scenes we ever animated.

Steve: One of my favorite scenes of all time was when Snoopy dances at the piano, as Schroeder plays those WWI songs.

Bill: That too was a great scene. I remember Sparky really liked that one.

Steve: Many of Snoopy's mannerisms always remind me of you.

Bill: Yes, I think there's a lot of me in that scene. Frankie Smith and Bill Littlejohn [fellow animators] and I all contributed. Littlejohn was especially useful because he was a flier and very good with music as well. He also was a key to the success of the Red Baron sequence.

Steve: This was the first time you animated Lucy pulling away the football.

Bill: Yes, and, at first, we didn't know how to handle that. It was simpler to do it in the strip. But in animation, we had to be careful how we had him crash onto the ground, so it wasn't too painful to the TV viewers. We just covered the crash with a lot of dust and other animation effects. But it was a lot of fun having him fly through the air when Lucy pulled the ball.

Steve: This show had a lot more color than the first two shows.

Bill Melendez looking at storyboards, 1975

Bill: With all the great color of the fall season and the pumpkin patch, we were able to go to watercolors for the first time. The colors were really vivid. Our first two shows were flat. But we had to go to what we called dimensional space on the drawing board, especially in the pumpkin patch. And then Dean Spille [another artist who worked on the show] did those great color backgrounds. This was the first show that we were able to do all this.

Steve: We never see the Red Baron after he gets shot down by Snoopy.

Bill: Well, that's the fun of the fantasy of the whole thing. It's like we never see the opposing baseball team in *Charlie Brown's All Stars!*—it's all taken over by the imagination of the viewer. In reality, of course, there is no Red Baron.

Steve: There's a great musical score throughout.

Bill: Well, Vince wrote some great music, as he did on all the shows. "The Great Pumpkin Waltz" and the "Red Baron Theme" were perfect for those scenes. You know Vince had very short stubby fingers, and I was always amazed at how he would attack the piano and create that wonderful music.

Steve: The last scenes in the pumpkin patch, where Sally is screaming at Linus, are so funny.

Bill: Fortunately, we had a great six-year-old actress named Cathy Steinberg who pulled it off. Her yelling was perfect to animate.

Steve: When this show came on for the first time in 1966, almost half of the viewers in America tuned in. And nearly forty years later it still wins its time period. Are you surprised by the longevity of the success of this show?

Bill: Well, I'll be ninety years old for the fortieth anniversary of the show. Who would have thunk it? I have always been very proud of *Pumpkin*. It's probably one of the best shows we ever created. It allowed us to really break out, for the first time, with great animation, from the kicking of the football to the Red Baron. I'm very gratified by the good ratings after all these years. I noticed this week we were even number one with viewers eighteen to forty-nine, not just the children. The adults of today were the kids of yesterday who watched the show and still do. That's really something.

WHERE DID THE "FLYING ACE" COME FROM?

If the scenes with Snoopy as the Flying Ace chasing the Red Baron helped to make *Pumpkin* a blockbuster, and if that helped us to do dozens of more shows, who gets the credit for the original idea?

As I mentioned earlier, Sparky had said he thought he could claim credit, but his son Monte remembered things differently. So I recently called Monte to give him "equal time," and this was his response:

"What I remember was that I was building model airplanes at the time and I really got into WWI planes. I knew a lot about them and had built a Sopwith Camel and a Fokker Triplane. I wandered into Dad's studio one afternoon and suggested, like a kid does, that it would be a good idea to have Snoopy, in his imagi-

nation, either fighting WWI airplanes or fighting the Red Baron. I can't remember exactly what my suggestion was, but it was something to that effect. And Dad, as I recall, was not overly enthused about the idea. He sort of smiled and went back to the strip he was working on that day. It was more than a week later—perhaps a few weeks—when he showed me a Sunday strip he had completed. He included Snoopy flying his Sopwith Camel, or rather his doghouse, in pursuit of the Red Baron.

"He actually let me color the panel of a copy that he had, letting me think this was the actual strip he would be sending off to the syndicate, because the Red

Baron thing had been mine. Somewhere over the years I lost that strip and losing it somehow was like losing the Smoking Gun. It was my proof that the thing had been my idea. Why? That was the only strip he ever let me color!

"Years later when I heard Dad tell someone that he thought he had come up with the idea himself, I was shocked! Of course, everything in the future strips— the jokes, the root beer, etc.—*were* Dad's, but I maintain that the first thought of having Snoopy fly the WWI plane was my idea!"

Well Monte, I am here to set the record straight. One day when I was visiting Sparky after he had retired, just before his passing, we started talking about a bunch of different things. We got to talking about the fact that he never took ideas from anyone for the comic strip, though he did make rare exceptions for his family. For example, when his son Craig was into helicopters and motocross racing, those themes not only filtered into the comic strip but also into our TV shows. Daughters Meredith, Amy, and Jill also gave him ideas from time to time as they were growing up. His wife, Jeannie, gave him the idea of Sally calling Linus her "Sweet Baboo."

Of course the issue of the Red Baron popped into my mind. We had talked about it before, and there had always been some controversy surrounding it. So I asked, "What do you think? Many years ago you said that Monte thought he came up with the idea of the Flying Ace and the Red Baron, but you felt that you came up with the idea yourself."

After thinking a few moments Sparky replied, "You know . . . looking back and thinking about what Monte was doing around that time with all those model airplanes, maybe it was Monte's idea after all." He paused, then added, "But I *drew* it!!" And finally he laughed at how he had reacted.

Just a few months after the Flying Ace first appeared in the comic strip in early 1966, it found its way into the *Great Pumpkin*. And look where it went from there:

1. A drawing of Snoopy as the Flying Ace was flashed from outer space by the astronauts on *Apollo 10*.
2. There's been an exhibit of the Flying Ace and the Red Baron in the Smithsonian National Air and Space Museum for many years.
3. The Flying Ace even became a U.S. postage stamp!

So that's just how far a single idea can fly!!!

CHARLES M. SCHULZ

The first time I met Sparky was in 1963, when we started filming a documentary about him and his characters. Some of the things that he said off and on camera have stayed with me to this day:

"I have a very small 'overhead.' It's just this desk . . . a few pens and pencils . . . and the paper I draw on. Isn't that great?" he said once and laughed.

"When I was in grammar school, I skipped ahead a few grades. Suddenly I was the shortest, skinniest, and youngest kid in my class. So I was picked on all the time. That's why I have always been against bullying of any kind . . . at any level. So I guess part of the whole thing with the comic strip is Charlie Brown being picked on all the time and yet he survives . . . he keeps on trying. I assume a lot of people can identify with that."

"All I do is draw funny pictures. That's it."

Charles Schulz working at his desk

"Somebody asked me what my philosophy is. And I told him it's to finish the strip and send it out before the post office closes."

"I think Charlie Brown is a real nice kid . . . someone you'd like to have as a neighbor."

"The comic strip is all about design and space. You only have four small panels to work with. So I have to write the script, create the sets, and direct the characters."

"It's what I love doing best, but it does take a toll. Because it's like having a term paper to do every single day. And the thing that scares me the most is that I will let down my readers on any given day. So that's my motivation . . . to be the very best I can be every single day."

I probably met with Sparky close to a thousand times during the nearly 40 years we worked together. And every time I entered his studio, the first thing he would do would be to hand me the comic strip he was working on, and he would ask me what I thought of it.

Although the strip was his daily and lifelong concern, he thoroughly enjoyed working on the TV shows. Most of the shows were created just like the *Great Pumpkin* meeting described earlier. After the initial meeting and the start of a script, Bill would develop the storyboard. We would meet again, and Sparky would develop even more of the script. The meetings for each special probably averaged once or twice a month over a period of six or seven months.

In all the time we worked together we never had a disagreement. I think that's because we each respected the other's "turf." Sparky thoroughly trusted Bill's animation and my direction of the children and music. There was never any second-guessing. Once one show was done, we just moved on to the next one.

We were just good friends. There are only half a dozen pictures of the three of us over four decades. We simply never bothered. We were having too much

fun to pose for cameras. The fact that we lived in three different cities probably was a good thing too . . . we weren't working in a Hollywood pressure cooker.

A majority of the early shows obviously came right from the comic strip. But Sparky was never adverse to adding original material as well. That made a very good mix. And another likely reason for our success was that the network left us almost completely alone, which is unheard of in our business. They would look at the storyboard, make a few suggestions (which were always ignored), and then wait for the final product.

I was thinking the other day that in all those times that we met, I never once asked for Sparky's autograph. I must have thought it would have been an intrusion on our friendship. However, I did receive a few surprises.

Back in 1971, I wrote about the following incident in a book called *Charlie Brown and Charles Schulz*, originally published by World Publications. It bears repeating here:

Sparky once pulled a trick on me. In a Sunday strip, Lucy knocks Charlie Brown's croquet ball away downtown. Charlie Brown goes to a pay phone booth and says: "Call me when it's my turn, will you? The number here is 343–2794 . . . "

Well, that's my home phone number. We hadn't read the strip, and we didn't know why we were getting dozens of calls. Most everyone would ask: "Is Charlie Brown there?"

But there were no area codes in those days. So many people had this same number in different states. People all over America were getting calls, and none of them had a clue why people were asking for Charlie Brown.

Late in the day, I answered the phone. This was the first time it had been an adult. "Is Charlie Brown there?"

I replied: "No Sparky, he's not. And stop laughing."

So everything we did on television and everything that emanated in different products around the world—including stage shows and books . . . everything came from the strip.

Sparky drew more than 18,000 of those strips! He never had an assistant and he once said, "That would be as if Arnold Palmer hit your nine iron for you." Just think of that . . . more than 18,000 comic strips.

And thank goodness for the comic strips about Linus in the Pumpkin Patch and Snoopy as the Flying Ace. Without them, we never could have created *It's the Great Pumpkin, Charlie Brown*. Or all the specials that followed.

Bar Sheets

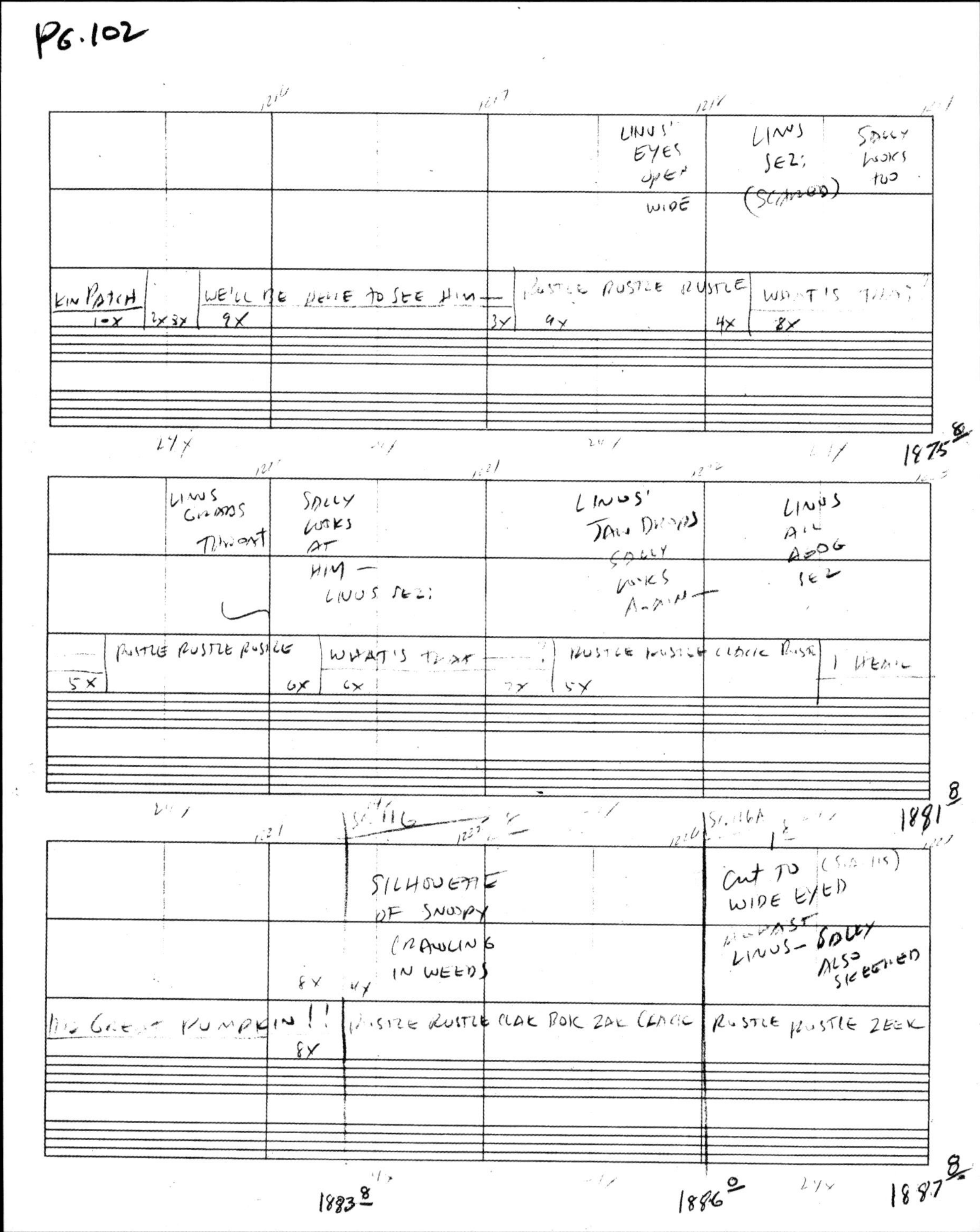

PG.102

					LINUS' EYES OPEN WIDE	LINUS SEZ: (SCARED)	SALLY LOOKS TOO
KIN PATCH		WE'LL BE HERE TO SEE HIM—		RUSTLE RUSTLE RUSTLE	WHAT'S THAT?		
1=X	2x 3x	9X		3X	9x	4X	8X

1975 $\frac{8}{}$

	LINUS GRABS THROAT	SALLY LOOKS AT HIM — LINUS SEZ:		LINUS' JAW DROPS SALLY LOOKS AGAIN		LINUS AGOG SEZ
	RUSTLE RUSTLE RUSTLE	WHAT'S THAT		RUSTLE RUSTLE CLACK RUSTLE		I HEAR
5X		6X	6x		7X	5X

1881 $\frac{8}{}$

		SILHOUETTE OF SNOOPY CRAWLING IN WEEDS				Cut TO (S.A. 115) WIDE EYED PAST LINUS—SALLY ALSO STARTLED
It's GREAT PUMPKIN!!		RUSTLE RUSTLE CLAK BOK ZAK CLACK				RUSTLE RUSTLE ZEEK
	8X	8X	4X			

1883 $\frac{8}{}$ 1886 $\frac{0}{}$ 1887 $\frac{8}{}$

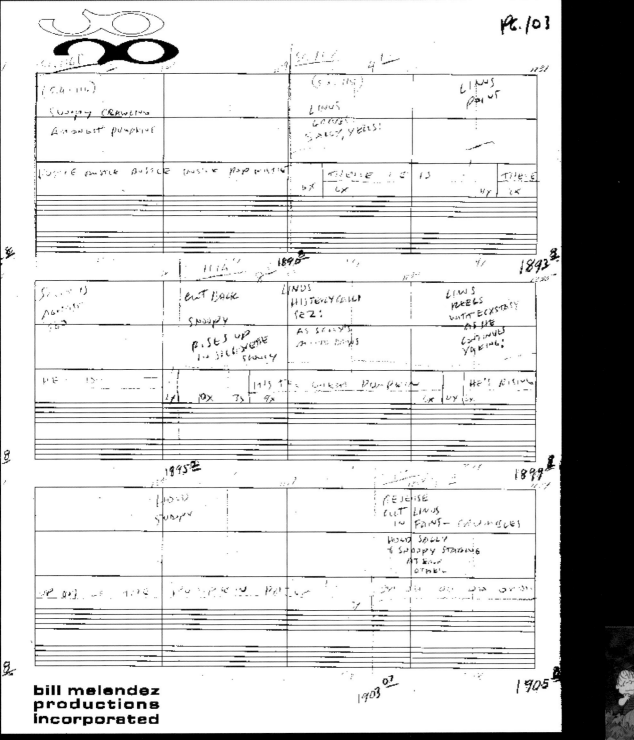

bill melendez
productions
incorporated

Route Sheet

PROD. No. 66-45   **TITLE** _____   **FILM** _____

Sc.	SCREEN FTG.	ANIM FTG.	ANIMATOR	ACTION	LAYOUT	BG's.	ANIM.	ASST.	FINAL TEST	CHKG.	I-P.	PROD. CAMERA	CUT.
1	21²	5	T.	KIDS LEAVE HOUSE ON WAY TO PUMPKIN PATCH	PAN	ED	X						
2	51²	10		KIDS WALK INTO PUMPKIN PATCH	PAN		X						
3	4²	1		KIDS WALK TO HOLE IN FENCE	STILL		X						
4	13²			LINUS ROLLS PUMPKIN AROUND FENCE	STILL		X						
5	4²	1		LINUS DUMPS PUMPKIN	PAN		X						
6	1⁴	1		LUCY WALKING - LINUS ENTERS	STILL		X						
7	4⁰	1		LUCY BY STEPS - LINUS IN	SA 5		X						
8				LINUS STOPPING - INTO SPIN									
9	1²	1		LUCY BY STEPS - LINUS ROLLS UP	STILL		X						
10	13⁸	2		LINUS' SPIRALS BY LUCY, GLARING	STILL		X						
11	9²	2		LUCY, LINUS PUMPKIN INTO HOUSE	STILL		X						
12	34⁸	7		LUCY CUTS UP PUMPKIN	STILL		X						
13	36¹²	7	FILL	SPOOKY LANDSCAPE - KIDS IN COSTUMES	PAN		X						
14	10²	1		1ˢᵗ TITLES COME ON	PAN		X						
15	3²	1		OWL HOOTS & FLIES OFF	STILL		X						
16	22²	3		SPONSOR CREDIT - GHOST & KIDS	PAN	R	X						
17	34⁸	7		SWAMPY BLOWING AT LEAVES	PAN	BERN	X						
18	12¹²	3		LINUS WITH SUCKER - LEAPS	PAN		X						
19	17¹²			LINUS LEAPS INTO LEAVES	PAN		X						
19-A	36		RUDY	C.S. LINUS YELLING	CARD		X						
20	8⁴	1		C.S. LUCY YELLING AT CHARLIE	SA 17		X						
21	10²			CHARLIE ANGRILY TALKS TO LUCY	CARD SA 19 A		X						
22	16¹²	3		C.S. LUCY HOLDING FOOTBALL	SA 17		X						
24	11²	L		CS CHARLIE TALKING	CARD SA 19A		X						
25	55⁸	11		LUCY WAVES DOCUMENT	STILL		X						
26				C.B. WALKING - READING DOCUMENT	PAN		X						
27	5¹²			LINUS WRITES TO "GREAT PUMPKIN"	CARD		X						
27-A	3⁸			C.S. CHARLIE ASKS:	SA 27		X						
28	10⁸		FRANK	LINUS TALKING TO CHARLIE SA 27	SA 27		X						
29	6⁶			CHARLIE INTERRUPTS LINUS	SA 27		X						
30	45⁶	10		LINUS WRITING	STILL		X						
31A	11⁴			LINUS IN DOOR - LUCY THROWS HIM OUT	SA 27		X						
33	63⁴	11		LINUS IN HOUSE - KIDS ENTER & LEAVE	SA 27		X						
34	3⁸			LINUS BLUSHING & COY 342:	SA 27		X						
35	10⁸	2	LITTLEJOHN	SALLY TALKS	SA 27		X						
36	7⁸			LINUS TALKING TO SALLY	SA 27		X						
37	24¹²	5	LITTLEJOHN	LINUS CAN'T QUITTING	JO 27		X						
38	7⁴			LUCY BY TV SET - LINUS ENTERS	SA 31		X						
39	21²	5	SEY	KIDS FOLLOW LINUS TO MAILBOX	PAN		X						
40	5¹²	1	ME	BLANKET WRINGS AROUND HAROLD	STILL		X						
41	7⁸		JERRIE	LINUS SAILS LETTER INTO BOX	STILL		X						
42	2⁴		ME	LETTER INTO BOX	STILL		X						
43	54⁰	12	LITTLEJOHN	LINUS DOES HAPPY DANCE	SA 41		X						
43-A	12⁸		JERRY B	LINUS EXITS PATCH	PAN		X						
44	12¹²	3		SALLY MAKING COSTUME	TEL	EV.	X						
45	10⁸	2		KIDS PREPARING FOR PARTY	PAN		X						
45-A	2⁴	1		LUCY DONS HAT & MASK	CARD		X						
45-B	57⁶	10		KIDS DON COSTUMES & TALKING	SA HS		X						
46	10²			SALLY DONS COSTUME	TEL		X						
				SALLY TALKING	TEL								
48	12¹²	2		CHARLIE DONS COSTUME	TEL		X						
49	8⁴			CHARLIE & SHEROOD ENTER	SA 45		X						
50	8⁴	1		CHARLIE LOOKS AT HIMSELF	STILL		X						
51	15²	3		C. & P. IN CLOUD OF DUST, WALKING	PAN		X						
52	4⁴	1		SWORD SWINGERS IN	STILL		X						

MUSIC USE SHEET

PROGRAM TITLE __IT'S THE GREAT PUMPKIN, CHARLIE BROWN__ *Show #3*

AIR DATE __10/27/66__ TIME_____ PRE-RECORDING DATE_____

TITLE OF COMPOSITION	TIME	COMPOSER	PUBLISHER	PERFORMERS	MANNER OF PRESENTATION
Pack Up Your Troubles in Your Old Kit Bag, Smile, Smile, Smile	:10	Arranged by Vince Guaraldi	Chappell	Vince Guaraldi Sextet	Background Instrumental
Roses of Picardy	:37	Arranged by Vince Guaraldi	Chappell	Vince Guaraldi Sextet	Background Instrumental
Great Pumpkin Waltz	:33	Vince Guaraldi	Shifty/Felfar BMI	Vince Guaraldi Sextet	Background Instrumental
Linus and Lucy	:14	Vince Guaraldi	Shifty/Felfar BMI	Vince Guaraldi Sextet	Background Instrumental
Linus and Lucy	:33	Vince Guaraldi	Shifty/Felfar BMI	Vince Guaraldi Sextet	Background Instrumental
Charlie Brown Theme	1:26	Vince Guaraldi	Shifty/Felfar BMI	Vince Guaraldi Sextet	Background Instrumental

Storyboards

...RUNS WILDLY TOWARD PILE ....

JUMPS UP IN HUGE LEAP - BLANKET TRAILING - CHARLIE → SNOOPY CRINGE ...

LINUS LANDS IN HUGE SCATTERING OF LEAVES

LINUS REAPPEARS LEAVES ARE STUCK ALL OVER HIS FACE CHARLIE → SNOOPY GLARE

LINUS (FACE ALL STUCK WITH LEAVES): NEVER JUMP INTO A PILE OF LEAVES WITH A ...

AS CHARLIE IS ABOUT TO LECTURE TO LINUS, LUCY ENTERS HOLDING FOOTBALL

bill meléndez productions incorporated

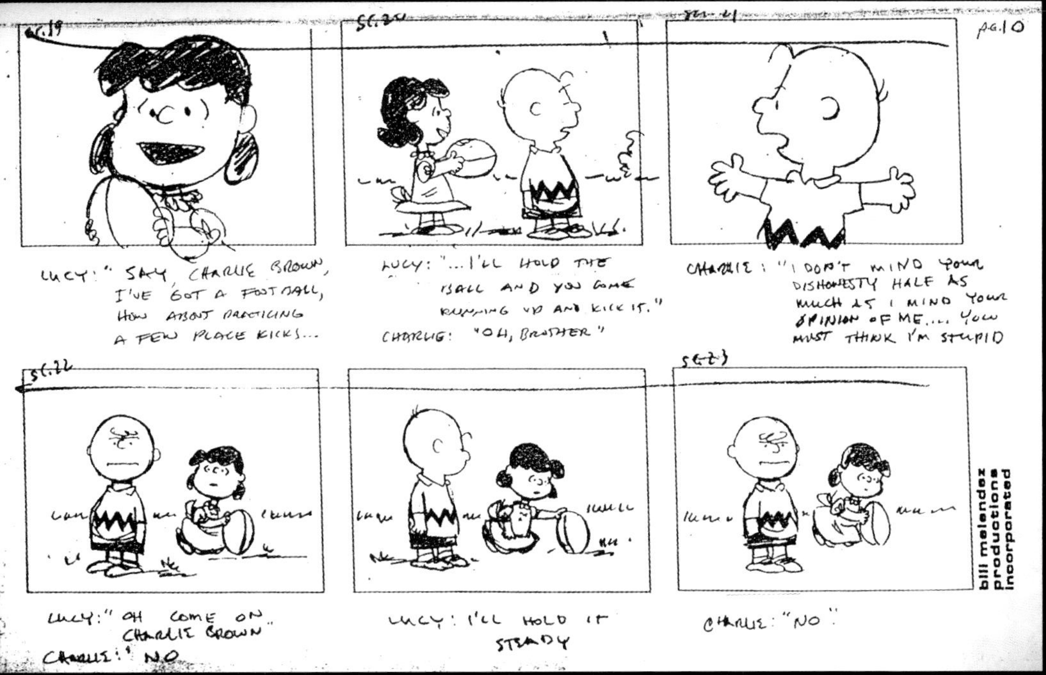
SC.19
SC.20
SC.21
PG.10
LUCY: "SAY, CHARLIE BROWN, I'VE GOT A FOOTBALL, HOW ABOUT PRACTICING A FEW PLACE KICKS...
LUCY: "...I'LL HOLD THE BALL AND YOU COME RUNNING UP AND KICK IT."
CHARLIE: "OH, BROTHER"
CHARLIE: "I DON'T MIND YOUR DISHONESTY HALF AS MUCH AS I MIND YOUR OPINION OF ME.... YOU MUST THINK I'M STUPID
SC.22
SC.23
LUCY: "OH COME ON. CHARLIE BROWN"
CHARLIE: " NO
LUCY: I'LL HOLD IT STEADY
CHARLIE: "NO"
bill melendez productions incorporated

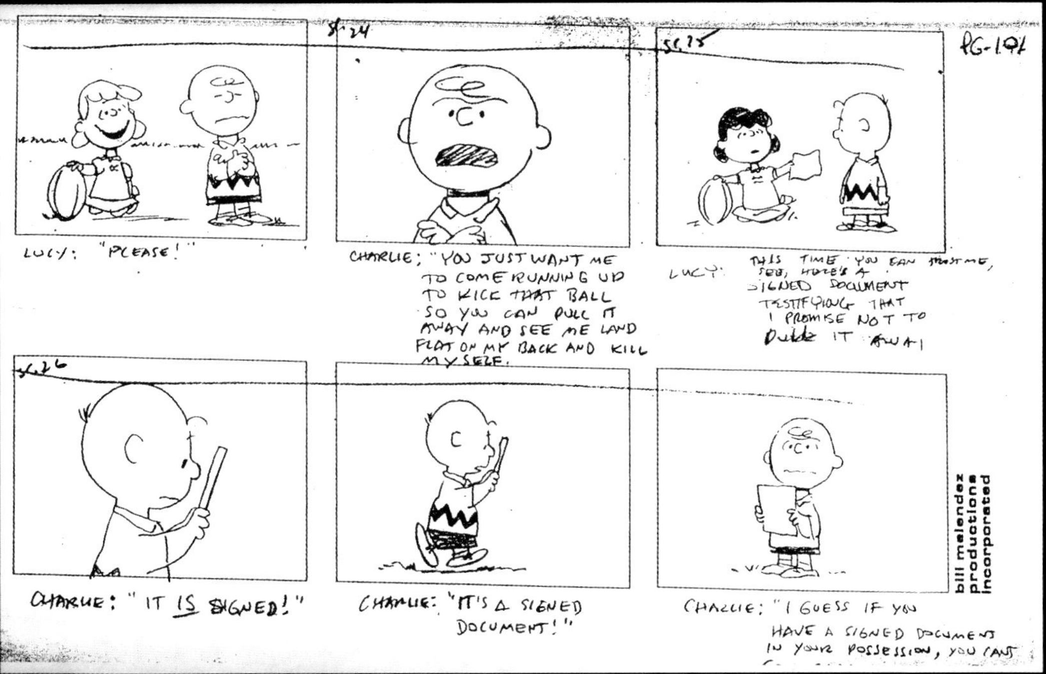
SC.24
SC.25
PG-10A
LUCY: "PLEASE!"
CHARLIE: "YOU JUST WANT ME TO COME RUNNING UP TO KICK THAT BALL SO YOU CAN PULL IT AWAY AND SEE ME LAND FLAT ON MY BACK AND KILL MYSELF.
LUCY: THIS TIME YOU CAN TRUST ME, SEE, HERE'S A SIGNED DOCUMENT TESTIFYING THAT I PROMISE NOT TO PULL IT AWAY
SC.26
CHARLIE: "IT IS SIGNED!"
CHARLIE: "IT'S A SIGNED DOCUMENT!"
CHARLIE: "I GUESS IF YOU HAVE A SIGNED DOCUMENT IN YOUR POSSESSION, YOU CAN'T
bill melendez productions incorporated

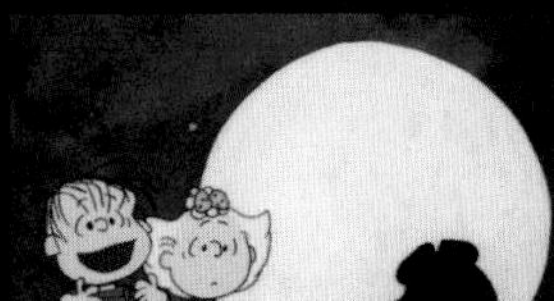

PG. 25

LINUS: "THE GREAT PUMPKIN KNOWS WHICH KIDS HAVE BEEN GOOD AND WHICH KIDS HAVE BEEN BAD, YOU'LL BE SORRY

LUCY: "OH GOOD GRIEF!"
LINUS: "HE'LL COME HERE BECAUSE I HAVE THE MOST SINCERE PUMPKIN PATCH AND HE RESPECTS SINCERITY."

SALLY TAKES OFF HER SHEET and asks wide eyed: "DO YOU REALLY THINK HE'LL COME?"

SC. 57

LINUS IMMEDIATELY BRIGHTENS UP AND SEZ: "TONIGHT THE "GREAT PUMPKIN RISES OUT OF

LINUS: "HE FLIES THROUGH THE AIR AND BRINGS TOYS TO ALL THE

SALLY: "THAT'S A GOOD STORY..."

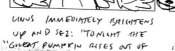

PG. 26

SALLY (AS SHE GETS A DOUBTFULL LOOK): I PLACE IT JUST A LITTLE BELOW THE ONE ABOUT THE FLYING REIN-DEER.

LINUS: "YOU DON'T BELIEVE THE STORY OF THE 'GREAT PUMPKIN'."

LINUS: I THOUGHT LITTLE GIRLS ALWAYS BELIEVED EVERYTHING THAT WAS TOLD TO THEM

LINUS (SADLY): I THOUGHT LITTLE GIRLS WERE INNOCENT AND TRUSTING

SALLY: WELCOME TO THE TWENTIETH CENTURY.

LUCY (INTERRUPTS): "ALL RIGHT ONCE AND FOR ALL, ARE YOU COMING OR ARE YOU

PG 25

LINUS WATCHES THE KIDS
GO — SALLY FOLLOWS THEM

SALLY STOPS AND LOOKS
BACK AT LINUS

SALLY RUNS BACK TO
LINUS

SC.58D SA. C.U. 57

SC.59   SA. 57

LINUS: "I'M GLAD YOU
CAME BACK, SALLY

LINUS: "WELL JUST SIT HERE
IN THIS PUMPKIN PATCH
AND YOU'LL SEE THE
"GREAT PUMPKIN" WITH

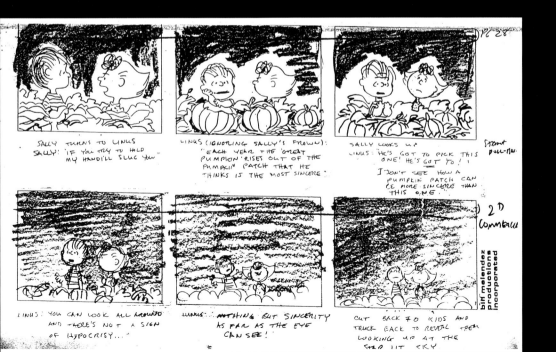

PG 28

SALLY TURNS TO LINUS
SALLY: "IF YOU TRY TO HOLD
MY HAND I'LL SLUG YOU"

LINUS (IGNORING SALLY'S FROWN):
"EACH YEAR THE 'GREAT
PUMPKIN' RISES OUT OF THE
PUMPKIN' PATCH THAT HE
THINKS IS THE MOST SINCERE"

SALLY LOOKS UP
LINUS: HE'S GOT TO PICK THIS
ONE! HE'S GOT TO!
I DON'T SEE HOW A
PUMPKIN PATCH CAN
BE MORE SINCERE THAN
THIS ONE.

START
PULL-BACK

) 2D
COMMERCIAL

LINUS: YOU CAN LOOK ALL AROUND
AND THERE'S NOT A SIGN
OF HYPOCRISY..."

LINUS: NOTHING BUT SINCERITY
AS FAR AS THE EYE
CAN SEE!

CUT BACK TO KIDS AND
TRUCK BACK TO REVEAL THEM
LOOKING UP AT THE
STAR LIT SKY

THE GREAT PUMPKIN WALTZ

By VINCE GUARALDI

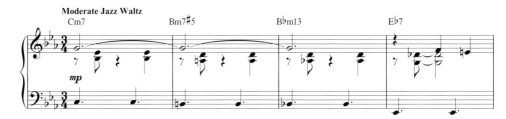

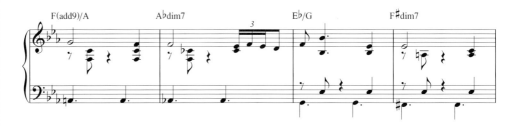

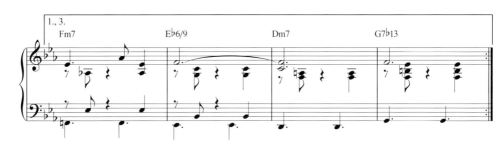

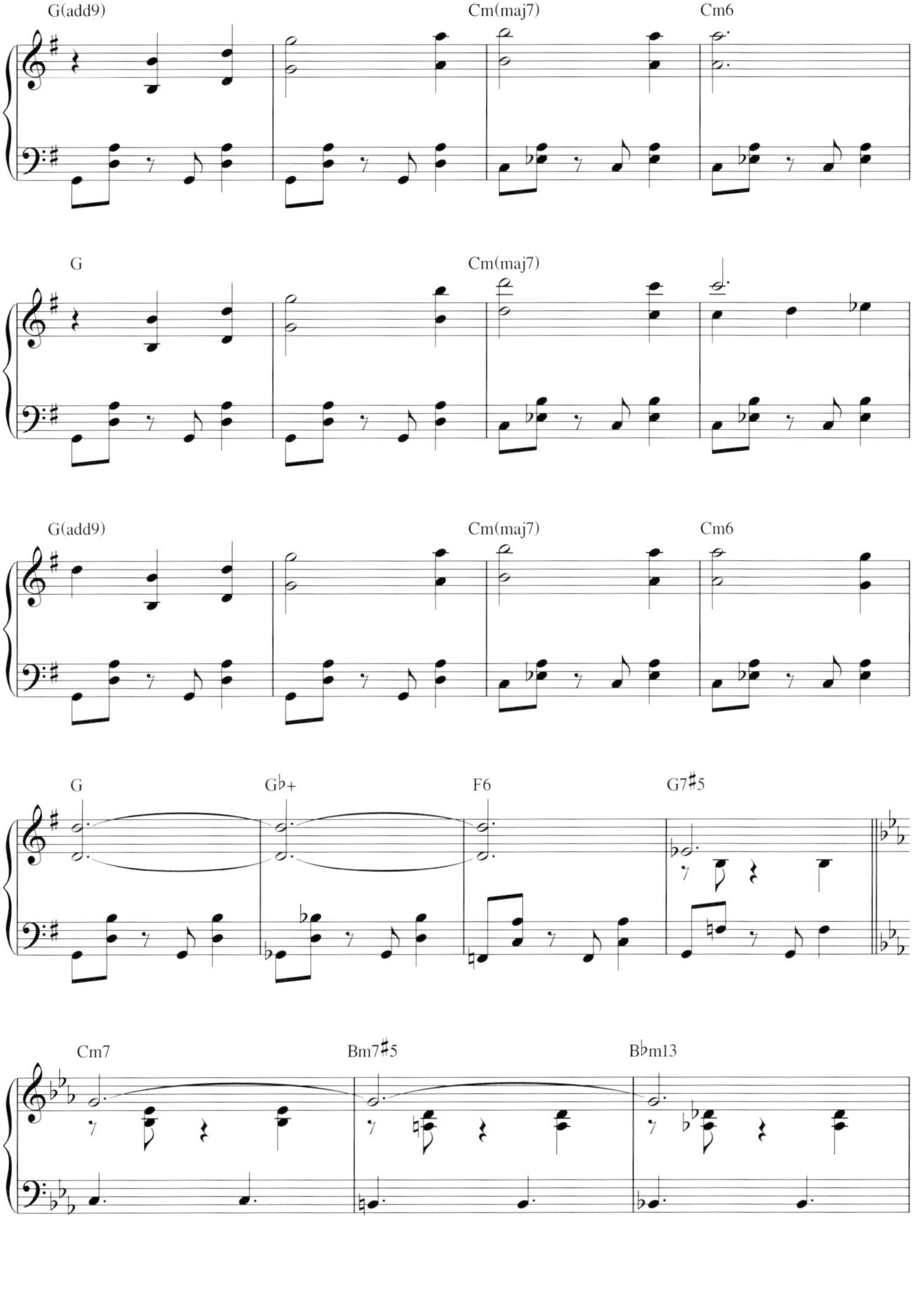
G(add9)
Cm(maj7)
Cm6
G
Cm(maj7)
G(add9)
Cm(maj7)
Cm6
G
G♭+
F6
G7♯5
Cm7
Bm7♯5
B♭m13

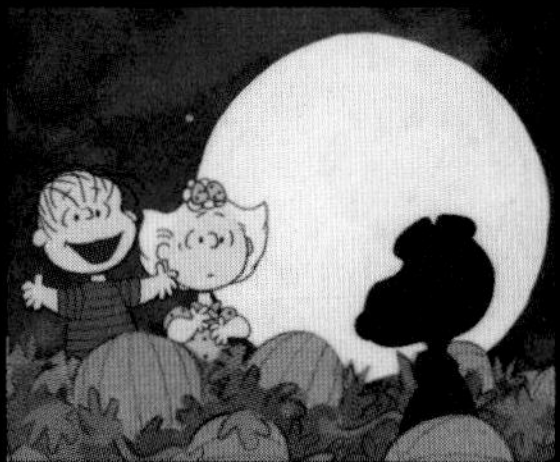

ORIGINAL PRODUCTION MATERIALS

Music by Vince Guaraldi

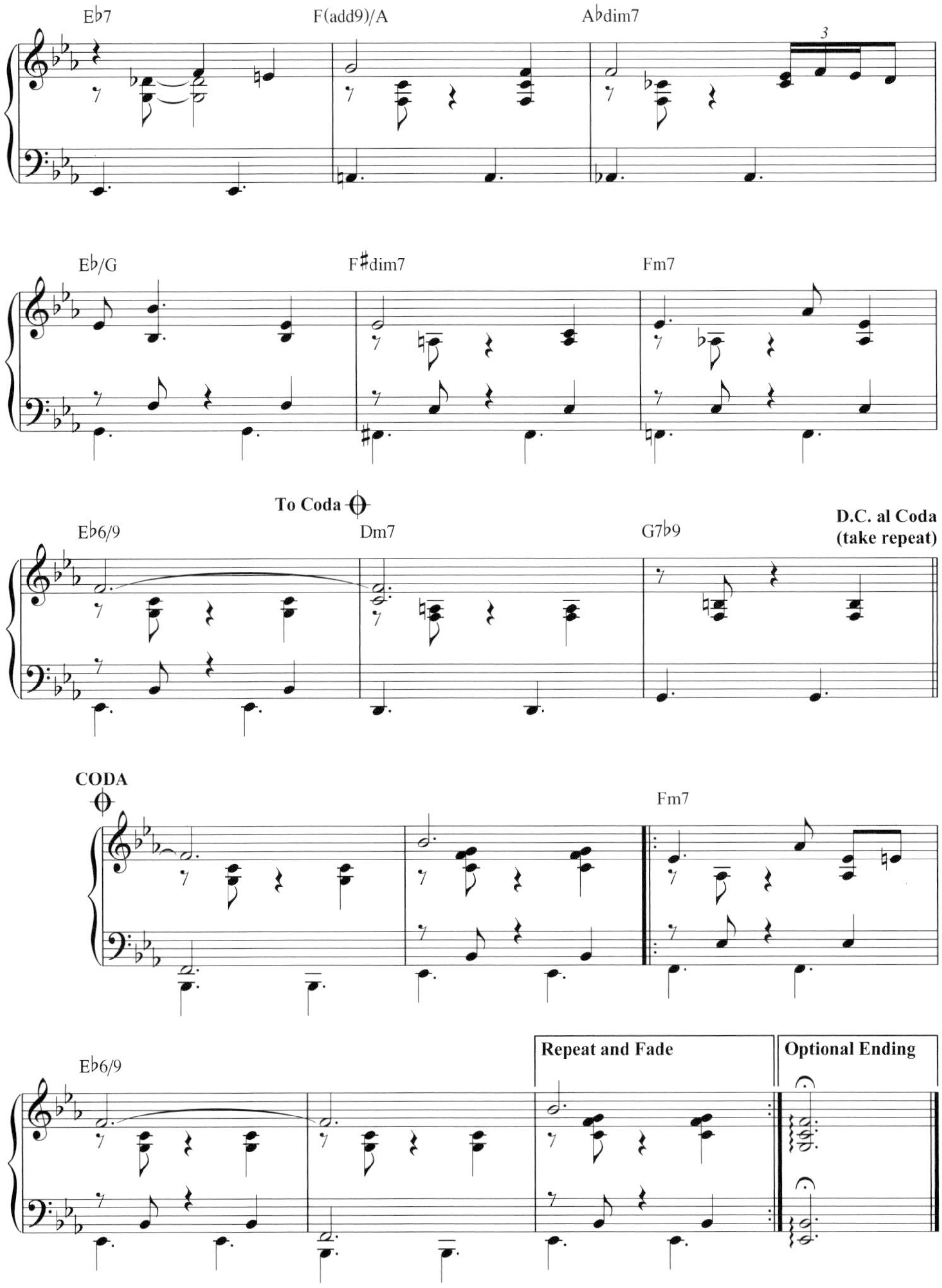

E♭7
F(add9)/A
A♭dim7
3
E♭/G
F♯dim7
Fm7
To Coda
E♭6/9
Dm7
G7♭9
D.C. al Coda
(take repeat)
CODA
Fm7
E♭6/9
Repeat and Fade
Optional Ending

RED BARON

By VINCE GUARALDI

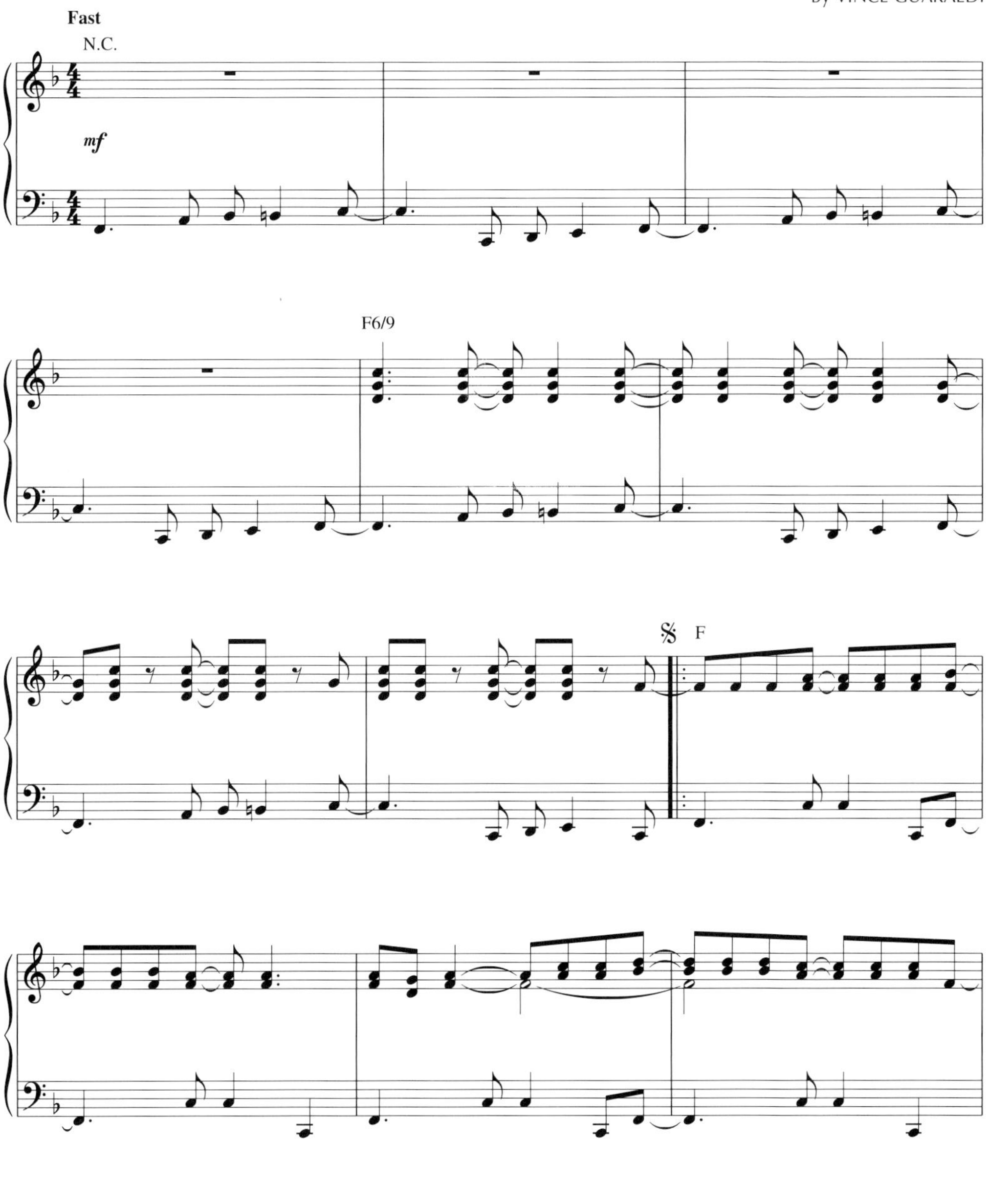
Fast
N.C.
mf
F6/9
F

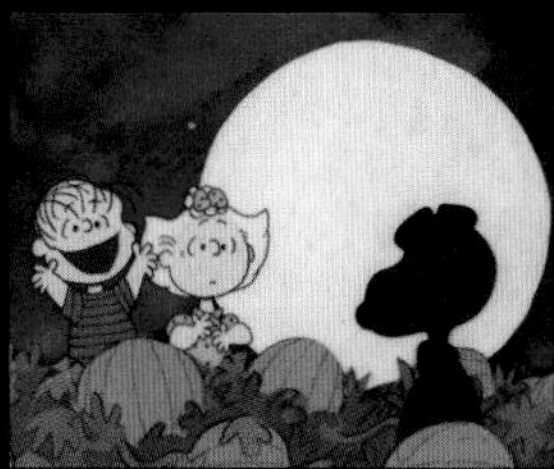

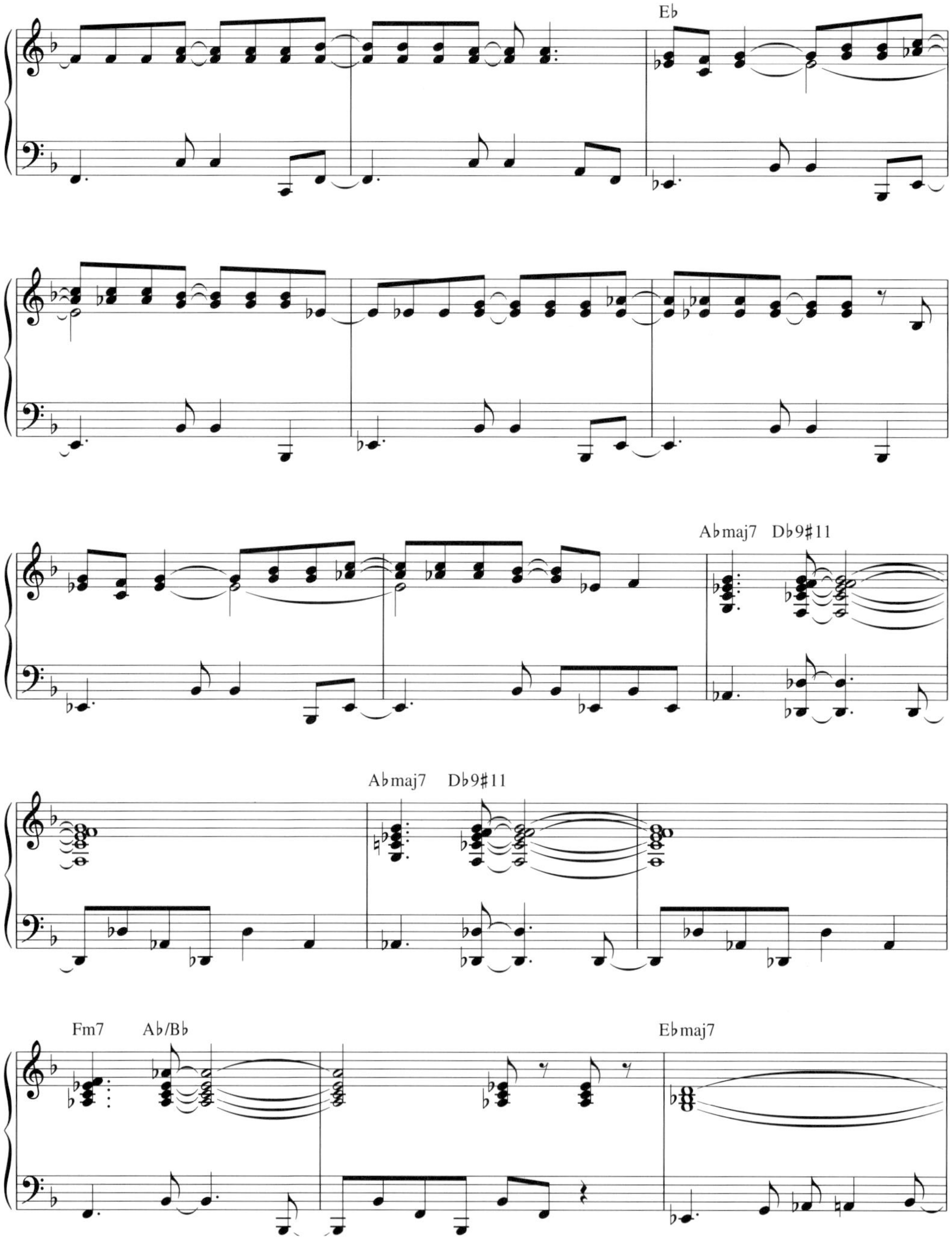
E♭
A♭maj7 D♭9♯11
A♭maj7 D♭9♯11
Fm7 A♭/B♭
E♭maj7

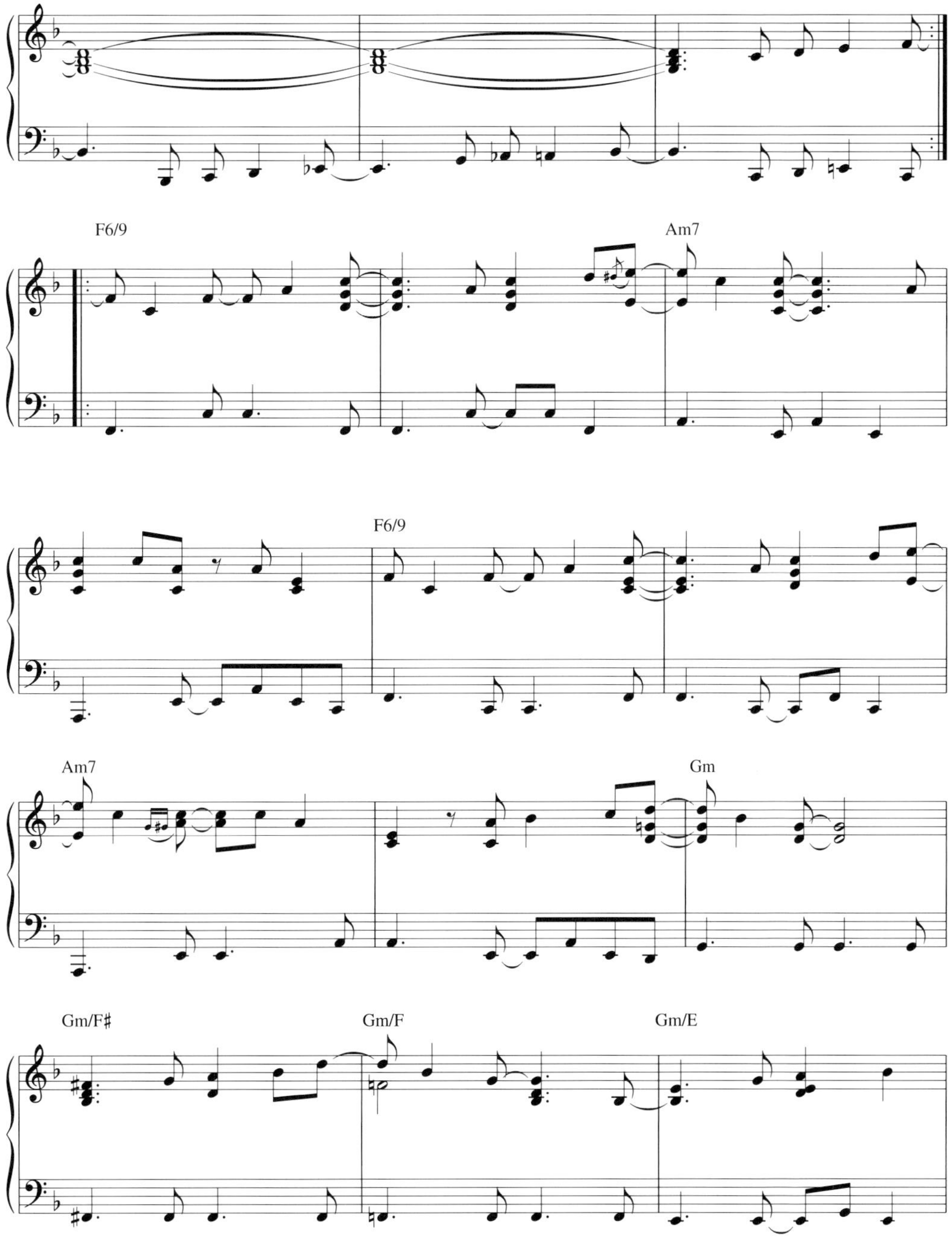
F6/9
Am7
F6/9
Am7
Gm
Gm/F♯
Gm/F
Gm/E
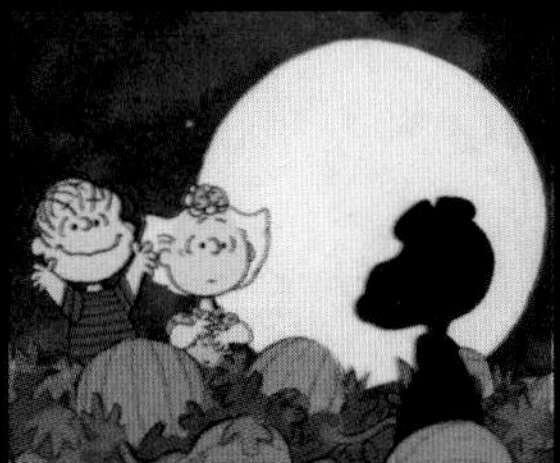

Music by Vince Guaraldi

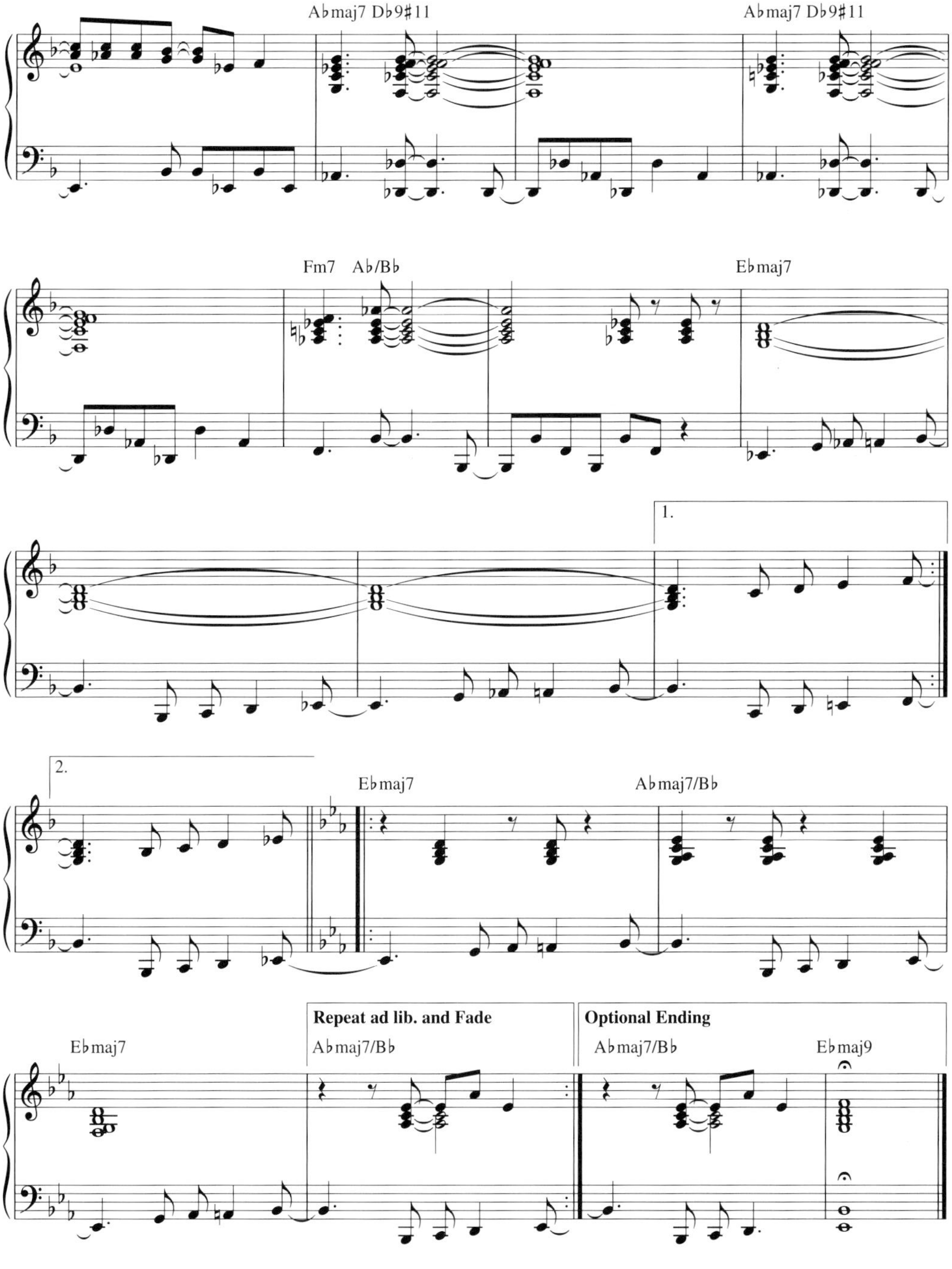
Abmaj7 Db9#11
Abmaj7 Db9#11
Fm7 Ab/Bb
Ebmaj7
1.
2.
Ebmaj7
Abmaj7/Bb
Ebmaj7
Repeat ad lib. and Fade
Abmaj7/Bb
Optional Ending
Abmaj7/Bb
Ebmaj9

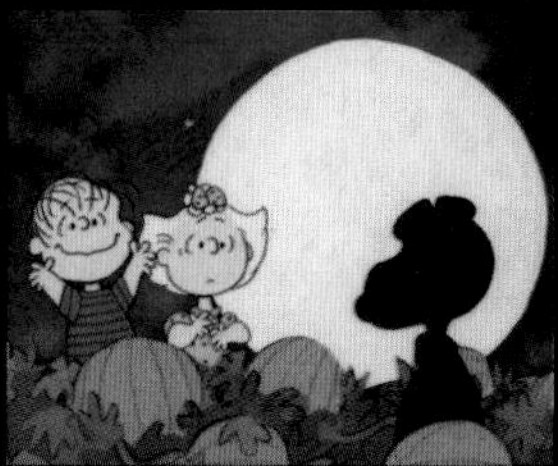

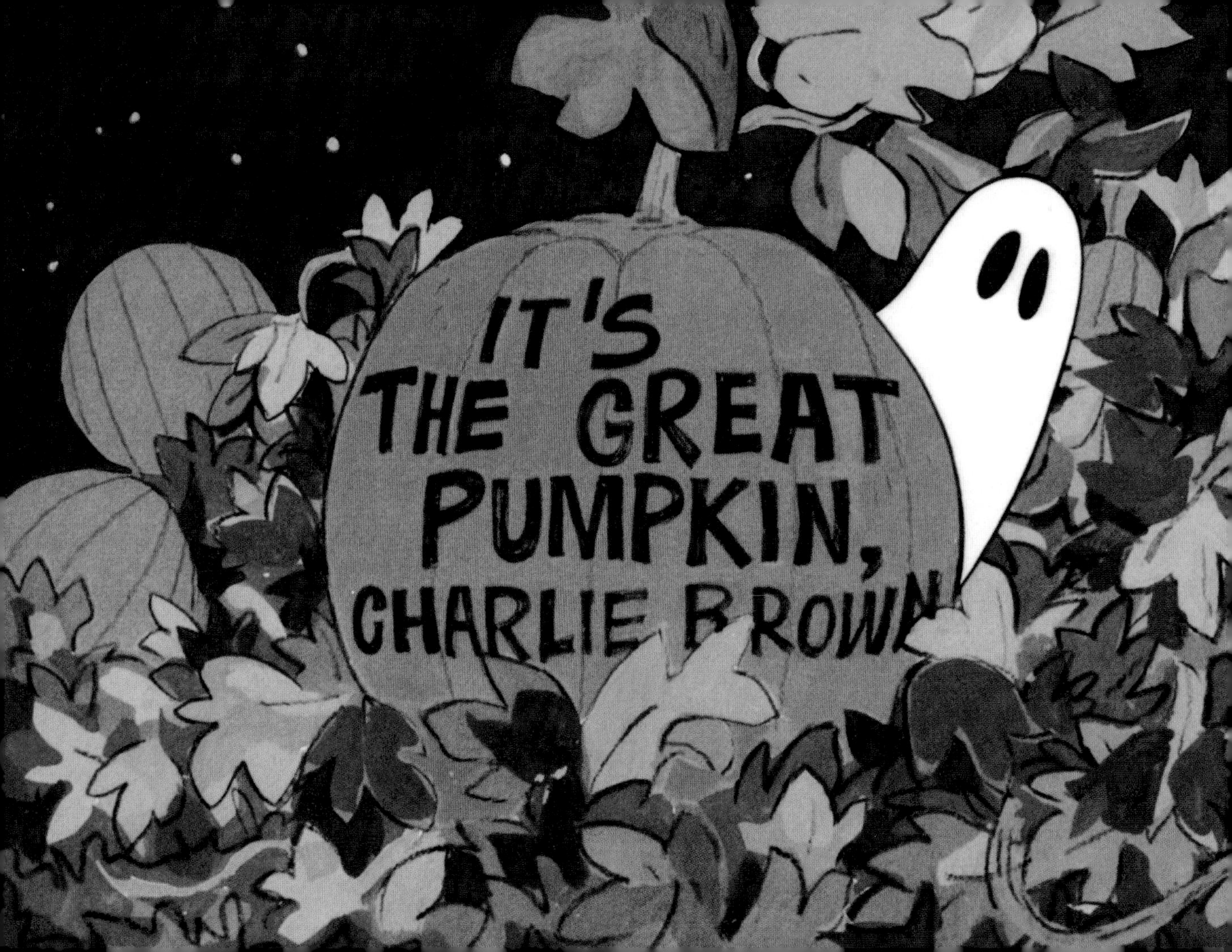
IT'S
THE GREAT
PUMPKIN,
CHARLIE BROWN

"IT'S THE GREAT PUMPKIN, CHARLIE BROWN"

THE ILLUSTRATED SCRIPT

The show opens with a prelude scene accompanied by the song "Linus and Lucy," composed and created by Vince Guaraldi. Exterior shot; it's a beautiful fall afternoon. Linus and Lucy take a walk to the pumpkin patch.

Linus selects one pumpkin, then another, but Lucy isn't satisfied.

Lucy points to the pumpkin she wants.

It's the biggest one in the pumpkin patch.

Linus struggles to carry it. The pumpkin won't fit through the hole in the fence so he rolls it home.

Soon the pumpkin is rolling Linus!

They bring the pumpkin inside.

Lucy begins to cut it open.

LINUS

You didn't tell me you were going to kill it!!!!

Fade to a night scene with trick-or-treaters in costume.

Different spooks come out to haunt them. They are chased by a ghost-like witch into the pumpkin patch where the title and credits are shown. An owl hoots and the screen fades to black.

Fade into daylight. Charlie Brown is raking leaves. Snoopy helps him by blowing a leaf onto the top of the pile.

CHARLIE BROWN
Thanks, old pal.

Linus comes running over and jumps in Charlie Brown's pile.

LINUS

Charge! Never jump into a pile of leaves with a wet sucker.

Enter Lucy.

LUCY

Say, Charlie Brown, I've got a football. How about practicing a few place kicks. I'll hold the ball and you come running and kick it.

CHARLIE BROWN

Oh, brother. I don't mind your dishonesty half as much as I mind your opinion of me . . . You must think I'm stupid.

LUCY
Oh come on, Charlie Brown.

CHARLIE BROWN
No.

LUCY
I'll hold it steady.

CHARLIE BROWN
No.

LUCY
Please.

CHARLIE BROWN
You just want me to come running up to kick that ball so you can pull it away and see me land flat on my back and kill myself.

LUCY
This time you can trust me . . . See, here is a signed document testifying that I promise not to pull it away.

CHARLIE BROWN

It's a signed document. I guess if you have a signed document in your possession you can't go wrong . . . This year I'm really going to kick that football!!

Charlie Brown falls on his back with a thud.

CHARLIE BROWN

Augh!

LUCY

Peculiar thing about this document . . . it was never notarized!!

Fade to Linus writing a letter to the Great Pumpkin.

LINUS
Dear Great Pumpkin, I am looking forward to your arrival on Halloween night.

Enter Charlie Brown.

I hope you will bring me lots of Halloween presents.

CHARLIE BROWN
Who are you writing to, Linus?

LINUS
This is the time of year to write to the Great Pumpkin. On Halloween night the Great Pumpkin rises out of his pumpkin patch and flies through the air with his bag of toys for all the children.

CHARLIE BROWN

You must be crazy. When are you going to stop believing in something that isn't true . . .

LINUS

When *you* stop believing in the fellow in the red suit and the white beard who goes, ho ho ho!

CHARLIE BROWN

We are obviously separated by denominational differences.

Charlie Brown exits.

LINUS

You must get discouraged because more people
believe in Santa Claus than in you.

Snoopy enters.

Well, let's face it . . . Santa Claus has had more
publicity. But being number two, perhaps you
try harder.

Snoopy laughs at Linus and exits.

Lucy enters.

LUCY

Not again!! Writing a letter to a stupid pumpkin?? You make me the laughing stock of the neighborhood. All they talk about is my little brother who always writes to the Great Pumpkin. You better cut it out now or I'll pound you!!

Lucy exits.

LINUS

There are three things that I've learned never to discuss with people. Religion, politics, and the Great Pumpkin!!

Patty enters.

PATTY

You're wasting your time. The Great Pumpkin is a fake.

Patty exits.

LINUS

Everyone tells me you are a fake, but I believe in you. P.S. If you really are a fake, don't tell me. I don't want to know.

SALLY

What are you doing, Linus?

LINUS

I'd rather not say, you might laugh!!

SALLY

Oh, I'd never laugh at you Linus, you're so intelligent.

LINUS

I'm writing to the Great Pumpkin.

SALLY

You say the cutest things.

LINUS

On Halloween night the Great Pumpkin rises out of the pumpkin patch and flies through the air to bring toys to all the good little children everywhere. Would you like to sit with me in the pumpkin patch on Halloween night and wait for the Great Pumpkin?

SALLY

Oh, I'd love to Linus.

Charlie Brown enters.

CHARLIE BROWN

What's going on here. What are you trying to do to my little sister?

Charlie Brown grabs Sally's hand and they exit.

Linus seals his letter and walks out of the house with his blanket.

LUCY

And how do you think you're going to mail that letter?

Lucy follows him to the mailbox.

LUCY

You can't possibly reach the mailbox and I'm not going to help you.

Linus whips his blanket around the handle of the mailbox and yanks it open.
With a flick of the wrist he launches the letter into the air. It floats up and slips
effortlessly into the mailbox.

Linus exits and Charlie Brown enters.

CHARLIE BROWN

Hey! I got an invitation to a Halloween party.

Charlie Brown dances with happiness.

LUCY

Is it the invitation to Violet's party, Charlie Brown?

CHARLIE BROWN

Yes, it's the first time I've ever been invited to a party!!

He continues to dance.

LUCY

Charlie Brown, if *you* got an invitation it was a mistake. There were *two* lists, one to invite, one not to invite. You must have been put on the wrong list.

Lucy exits and Linus enters carrying a sign that reads "Welcome Great Pumpkin." He walks past Charlie Brown into the pumpkin patch. Fade to black.

Open to a new scene. Sally is cutting holes in a sheet to make a costume. She holds it up and spooks herself.

Cut to Lucy, Violet, and Charlie Brown.

LUCY

A person should always choose a costume which is in direct contrast to her own personality.

Lucy puts on her witch mask. Sally enters.

SALLY

Is Linus taking me to the party?

LUCY

That stupid blockhead of a brother of mine is out in the pumpkin patch making his yearly fool of himself.

VIOLET

Boy, is he strange!

SALLY

But maybe there is a Great Pumpkin.

VIOLET

Every year Linus misses tricks or treats and then the party.

CHARLIE BROWN

He'll never learn.

SALLY

Do I get to go trick-or-treating this year, big brother?

CHARLIE BROWN

Sure Sally.

SALLY

Oh boy . . . oh boy . . . oh boy . . . How do we do it?

LUCY

All you have to do is walk up to a house, ring the doorbell, and say "tricks or treats."

SALLY

Are you sure it's legal?

LUCY

Of course it's legal.

SALLY

I wouldn't want to be accused of taking part in a rumble.

They all put on their costumes, including Charlie Brown, whose ghost costume is full of holes.

LUCY

Oh, good grief!

Enter Shermy and Schroeder..

SHERMY

Is that you, Patty?

LUCY

No.

SCHROEDER

Where is Charlie Brown?

CHARLIE BROWN

Here I am. I had a little trouble with the scissors.

Pigpen enters in a cloud of dust and dirt and says to himself:

PIGPEN

They'll never guess it's me under here.

SALLY

Hello Pigpen, glad you could make it.

PIGPEN

How did you know it was me?

Snoopy enters.

LUCY

What in the world kind of costume is *that*?

CHARLIE BROWN

He's a World War I Flying Ace.

LUCY

Now I've heard everything. All right everybody, now we'll go trick-or-treating
and then over to Violet's for the big Halloween party.

They walk out into the pumpkin patch.

LINUS

Hey, have you come to sing
pumpkin carols?

LUCY

You blockhead, you're going to miss
all the fun just like last year.

LINUS

Don't talk like that! The
Great Pumpkin knows which
kids have been good, and
which kids have been bad . . .
you'll be sorry.

LUCY

Oh good grief!

LINUS

He'll come here because I have the most sincere pumpkin patch and he respects
sincerity.

SALLY

Do you really think he'll come?

LINUS

Tonight the great pumpkin rises out of the pumpkin patch and flies through the
air and brings toys to all the children of the world.

SALLY

That's a good story.

LINUS

You don't believe the story of the Great Pumpkin? I thought little girls always believed everything that was told to them. I thought little girls were innocent and trusting.

SALLY

Welcome to the twentieth century.

LUCY

All right. Once and for all are you coming or are you staying? We can't waste all night.

Everyone but Linus leaves the pumpkin patch. Sally changes her mind and turns back to join him.

LINUS

I'm glad you came back, Sally. We'll just sit here in this pumpkin patch and you'll see the Great Pumpkin with your own eyes!!!

SALLY

If you try to hold my hand I'll slug you.

LINUS

Each year the Great Pumpkin rises out of the pumpkin patch that he thinks is the most sincere. He's got to pick this one, he's got to! I don't see how a pumpkin patch could be more sincere than this one. You can look all around and there is not a sign of hypocrisy. Nothing but sincerity as far as the eye can see.

Zoom out on Sally and Linus in the pumpkin patch.

Fade in on Lucy and the kids walking up to a house.

KIDS

Tricks or treats, money or eats!

LUCY

Can I have an extra piece of candy for my stupid brother? He couldn't come with us because he's sitting in a pumpkin patch waiting for the Great Pumpkin. It's so embarrassing to have to ask for something extra for that blockhead Linus.

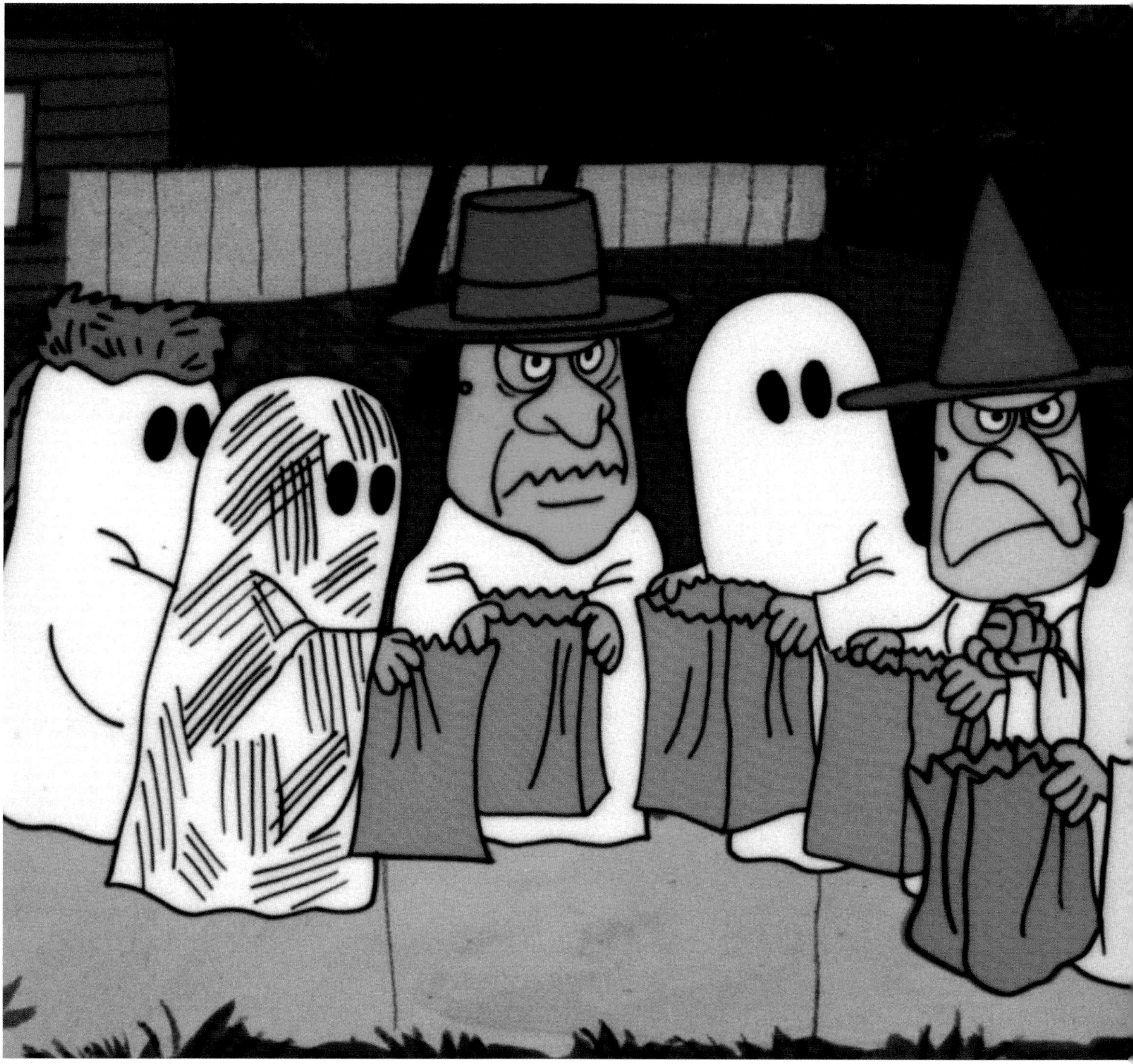

They open their bags to see what treats they've gotten.

LUCY

I got five pieces of candy.

VIOLET

I got a chocolate bar.

PATTY

I got a quarter.

CHARLIE BROWN

I got a rock.

KIDS

Tricks or treats!

VIOLET

Gee, I got a candy bar.

PATTY

Boy, I got three cookies.

LUCY

Hey, I got a pack of gum.

CHARLIE BROWN

I got a rock.

They walk up to another house.

LUCY

Tricks or treats. I got a popcorn ball!

PATTY

I got a fudge bar.

VIOLET

I got a package of gum.

CHARLIE BROWN

I got a rock.

They go to another house.

VIOLET

By the way . . . Whatever happened
to the World War I Flying Ace?

CHARLIE BROWN

Oh, he's probably getting ready to
take off in the Sopwith Camel on the
next dawn patrol.

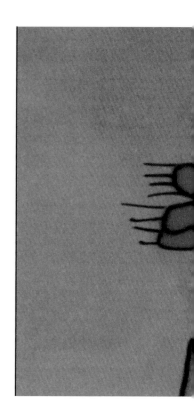

Cut to Snoopy dressed as the Flying Ace.

CHARLIE BROWN

His mission is to find the Red Baron and shoot him down. Here's the World War I Flying Ace climbing into the cockpit of his Sopwith Camel. "Contact," he shouts.

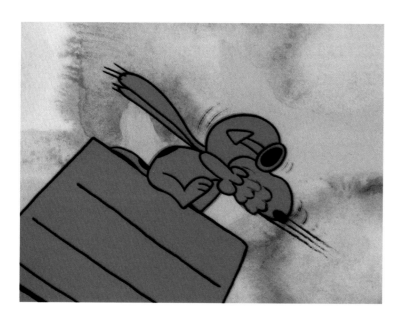

Snoopy takes off. He dodges gunfire. His doghouse is hit and he goes down.

CHARLIE BROWN

Here's the WWI Flying Ace imagining he's down behind enemy lines, making his way across the French countryside.

Fade back to the kids.

LUCY

C'mon. Let's get going. It's time for the Halloween party.

KIDS

Rayyyy . . .

On the way to the party the kids come across Sally and Linus, who are still waiting in the pumpkin patch.

VIOLET

Has the Great Pumpkin been by? Ha, ha, ha.

LUCY

What blockheads sitting in a pumpkin patch in the middle of the night!

PATTY

You've missed tricks or treats and now you're going to miss the Halloween party.

FRIEDA

What a way to spend Halloween!!

SALLY

You think you're so smart.
Just wait until the Great
Pumpkin comes. He'll be
here! You can bet on that!!
Linus knows what he's
talking about. Linus knows
what he's doing!!!

Sally turns to Linus.

All right, where is he?

LINUS

He'll be here . . .

SALLY

I hope so, I have my reputation
to think of, you know. And just
think of all the fun we're missing.

LINUS

Just look. Nothing but sincerity,
as far as the eye can see!

Fade to the party.

VIOLET

Charlie Brown, you'll have to model for us.

CHARLIE BROWN

Me? You want me to model?

PATTY

Sure, Charlie Brown. You'll be the perfect model.

LUCY

Turn him around.

Violet begins to draw on Charlie Brown's head.

VIOLET

If we shape the eyes like this, and the nose like this, and the mouth like this . . .

LUCY

Yes, that's the way. Thank you, Charlie Brown. You were the perfect model.

Meanwhile, the Flying Ace travels the
countryside, hiding under the cover of night.

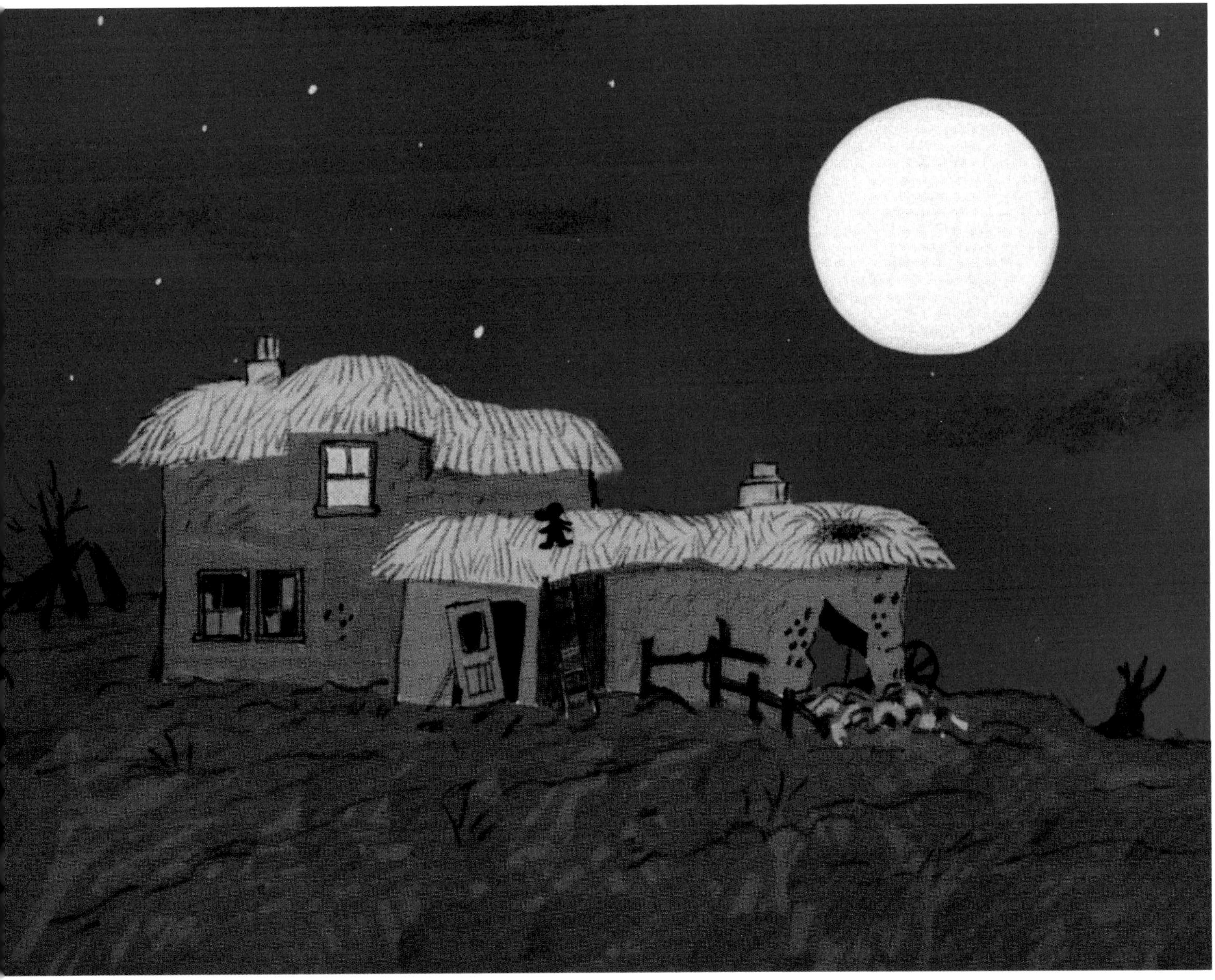

Fade back to the party.

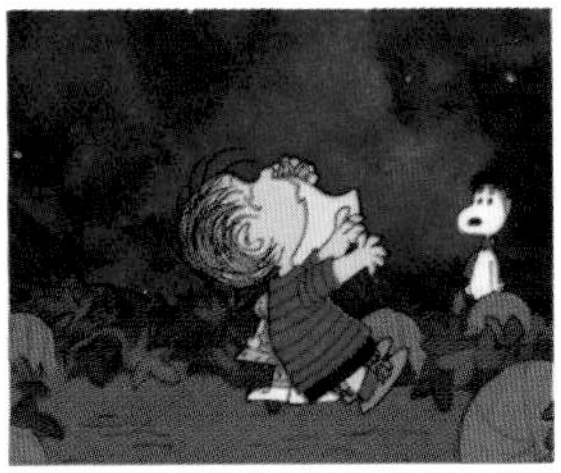

LUCY

All right . . . all right . . . let's bob for apples . . .

KIDS

Hooray! Great . . . let me at those apples.

LUCY

This is the way to do it!!

SCHROEDER

Yes, Lucy, you should be good at this since you have the mouth for it.

Lucy makes a face then plunges her head in the bucket of water.

LUCY

Bleah! My lips touched dog lips! Bleah, augh. Poison! Dog's lips. Bleah, augh.

Snoopy walks over to Schroeder, who plays some World War I songs, which have a profound effect on the Flying Ace. He marches, he conducts, and when the tune becomes sad he weeps. Snoopy exits the house crying and slips into the night.

Cut to Sally and Linus in the pumpkin patch.

SALLY

If anyone had told me I'd be waiting in the pumpkin patch on Halloween I'd have said they were crazy.

LINUS

Just think, Sally, when the Great Pumpkin rises out of the pumpkin patch we'll be here to see him. Was that?! Was that?! I hear the Great Pumpkin!

They see something move in the shadows.

There he is! There he is! It's the Great Pumpkin! He's rising out of the pumpkin patch. Ohhhhhhh!

Linus passes out and Sally can see that it's just Snoopy and not the Great Pumpkin after all.

LINUS

What happened?!! Did I faint? What did he leave us? Did he leave us any toys???

SALLY

I was robbed!!!!! I spent the whole night waiting for the Great Pumpkin when I could have been out for tricks or treats. Halloween is over and I've missed it!!!!

You blockhead! You kept me up all night waiting for the Great Pumpkin and all that came was a beagle!! And to think I didn't get to go out for tricks or treats. And it's all your fault! I'll sue!!!
What a fool I was! I could have had candy apples and gum and cookies and money and all sorts of things. But no! I had to listen to you! What a fool I was!

The rest of the kids enter at the end of Sally's speech.

Tricks or treats comes only once a year and I missed it by sitting in a pumpkin patch with a blockhead! You owe me restitution!!!

LINUS

You've heard about fury and a woman scorned, haven't you?

CHARLIE BROWN

Yes, I guess I have.

LINUS

Well that's nothing compared to the fury of a woman who has been cheated out of tricks or treats.

They all walk away, leaving Linus in the pumpkin patch.

LINUS

Hey, aren't you going to wait and greet the Great Pumpkin, huh? It won't be long now! If the Great Pumpkin comes I'll still put in a good word for you.

Good grief! I said "if." I meant *when* he comes. I'm doomed. One little slip like that could cause the Great Pumpkin to pass you by. Oh, Great Pumpkin, where are you . . .

Fade in on Lucy, who wakes up and realizes Linus is not in his bed. She walks to the pumpkin patch and finds Linus shivering. They walk back into the house and she helps get him into bed.

Fade to black.

Fade in on Charlie Brown and Linus.

CHARLIE BROWN

Well, another Halloween has come and gone.

LINUS

Yes, Charlie Brown.

CHARLIE BROWN

I don't understand it. I went trick-or-treating
and all I got was a bag full of rocks! I suppose
you spent all night in the Pumpkin Patch. And
the Great Pumpkin never showed up?

LINUS

Nope.

CHARLIE BROWN

Well, don't take it too hard, Linus. I've done a
lot of stupid things in my life too.

LINUS

Stupid?!?! What do you mean stupid?? Just wait
till next year, Charlie Brown. You'll see . . . Next
year at this same time. I'll find a pumpkin patch
that is real sincere.

And I'll sit in that pumpkin patch till the Great
Pumpkin appears . . .
He'll rise out of that pumpkin patch and fly
through the air with his bag of toys . . .

The Great Pumpkin will appear and I'll be
waiting for him . . . I'll be there.
I'll be sitting there in that pumpkin patch. And
I'll see the Great Pumpkin.

Fade out on Linus raving.

THE END

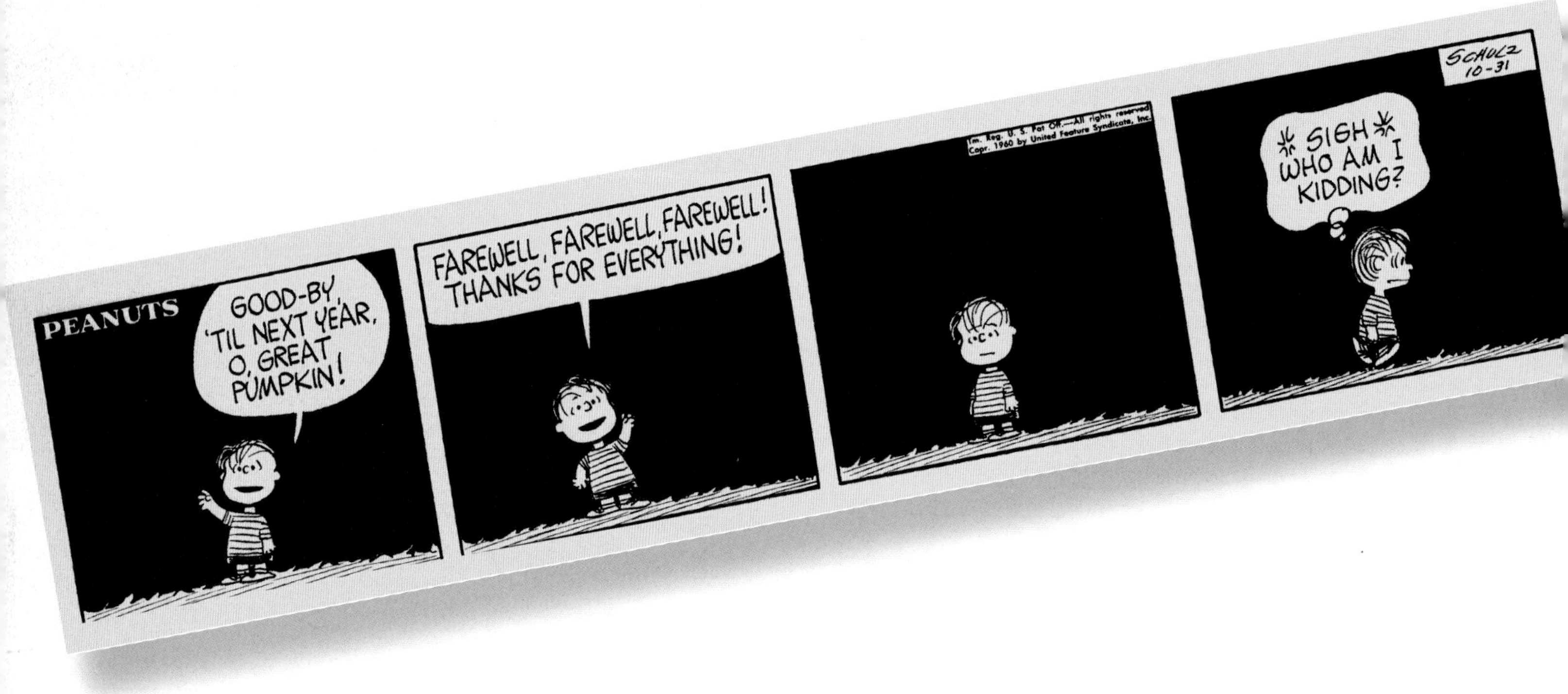
PEANUTS
GOOD-BY, 'TIL NEXT YEAR, O, GREAT PUMPKIN!
FAREWELL, FAREWELL, FAREWELL! THANKS FOR EVERYTHING!
Tm. Reg. U. S. Pat. Off.—All rights reserved
Copr. 1960 by United Feature Syndicate, Inc.
SCHULZ 10-31
SIGH WHO AM I KIDDING?

CREDITS

Directed by
Bill Melendez

Executive Producer: Lee Mendelson

Original Score composed and performed by Vince Guaraldi

Arranged and conducted by John Scott Trotter

Graphic blandishment by:
Ed Levitt, Bernard Gruerer, Frank Smith, Ruth Kissane, Dean
Spille, Bill Littlejohn, Beverly Robbins, Rudy Zamora, Elenor
Warren, Bob Carlson, Faith Kovaleski, John Freeman, Flora
Hastings

Voices:

Charlie Brown—Peter Robbins

Linus—Chris Shea

Lucy—Sally Dryer

Sally—Cathy Steinberg

Editing: Robert T. Gillis

Assisted by Steven Melendez

Sound by Producers' Sound Service

Camera: Nick Vasu

A Lee Mendelson—Bill Melendez Production

In cooperation with

United Feature Syndicate, Inc.

The End

It's the Great Pumpkin, Charlie Brown

© 1966 United Feature Syndicate, Inc.

"A CHARLIE BROWN™ CHRISTMAS"

The Making of a Tradition

SPECIAL 40TH ANNIVERSARY EDITION

THE MOST POPULAR CHRISTMAS TV SPECIAL OF ALL-TIME, "A Charlie Brown™ Christmas" is viewed every year by millions, young and old. The 40th Anniversary of this heartwarming, moving, often hilariously funny, and sophisticated animated cartoon will be marked by the publication of our four-color giftbook, *A Charlie Brown™ Christmas.*

❋ Original animation art
❋ Interviews
❋ The complete script
❋ Production notes
❋ Original score
❋ And much more!

This new edition of *A Charlie Brown™ Christmas* is a fitting salute to the artist who forever changed the face of cartooning.

HARPER